THE GIVE FIRST ECONOMY

How to Succeed In It.

KIRBY HASSEMAN

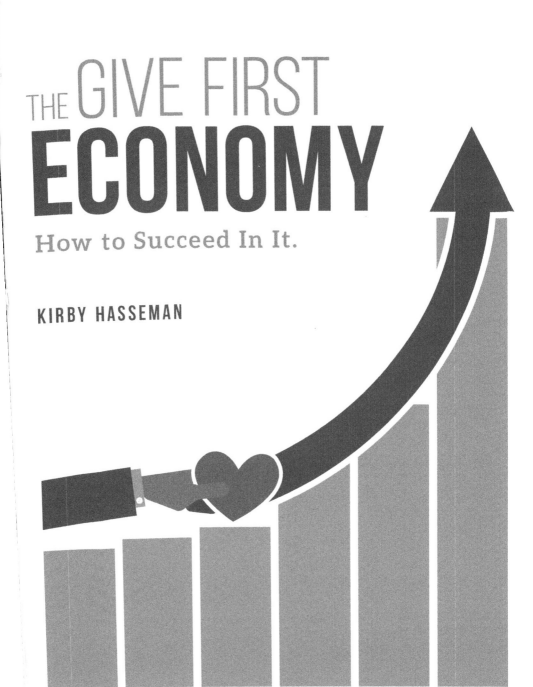

THE GIVE FIRST ECONOMY

How to Succeed In It.

KIRBY HASSEMAN

ACKNOWLEDGEMENTS

And now for the thank you's! I want to take just a moment to give credit to many people, without whom this book would not be possible.

My lovely bride *Amy Hasseman*...for continued and solid support.

My girls *Skylar and Jade*...for continued inspiration.

My parents *Rod and Chris* for helping me grow up...it was a tough job I know.

Thanks to the team at *Hasseman Marketing* for keeping things rolling.

Emily Bradford, Libbie Granger Prince, Jeff Wickerham, Jay Sabine, Kelly Bowe, Bree McAndrews, Eric Dingler, and Jim Duncan.

And a big thank you to *Josh Williams* for helping on layout and cover of the book. Amazing Job Josh.

Thanks to *Bill Petrie* for not only being a partner in podcasting, speaking and content...but also lending his voice to this book!

In addition, there have been countless others that have helped to inspire me and launch this book. Thanks so much to each of you!

PART 1
THE GIVE FIRST ECONOMY

You might be asking yourself a simple question, "who is this guy and why is he qualified to tell me how to "Succeed in the *Give First Economy*?" First, those are two questions, but I will let it pass. Second, I totally get it. I would be asking the same thing.

So, let me tell you a bit about me to kick this off.

I'm a sales guy and an entrepreneur. I started my first business at around 8 or 9 years old. It was a bike repair business and I got a client the very first day. Now this was before there was Facebook, so my parents couldn't do a "pity post" to get that account. I had to go out and give my puppy dog eyes door to door on my own. I got that pity sale the old-fashioned way - I begged!

Either way, I got back to my garage with my partner and realized something very quickly. I did NOT know how to fix bikes! So, I pivoted…and created a bike washing business!

I learned right away that I could sell. I also learned that you really needed to be able to back up your claims if you wanted to be in business for long!

When I was older and got into sales for a real career, I was the same way. I could sell. I was happy to get after it. I would park my car at a local industrial park and go door to door working hard to make as many sales as I could. I was happy to shake hands and kiss babies. I dropped off my flyers and learned all the sales tactics I could.

Why am I telling you this?

I simply want you to know that I am a sales guy at heart. I want results.

Several years ago, however, I started to notice something. The people that I admired and followed were doing things a bit differently. They were putting out content. They were sharing information freely. These people were pioneering the content world with videos, blogs, and even podcasts. I ate up the content and decided I wanted to be more like them.

I did not want to spend the rest of my life simply dropping off my catalogs and hoping someone would buy from me instead of the 100's of other competitors. I wanted to have people view me as the expert and call me when they needed my products and services.

So, I started to create content…and I was terrible at it. I created videos. I wrote random blogs. I tried and failed at many content forms. But I got better at it, and in 2014 I stumbled upon something that stuck.

I created a video show called *Delivering Marketing Joy* where I interviewed marketers, entrepreneurs, salespeople and more about their business, and I put out a brand-new episode every week! It was a huge undertaking, but the response was really good. So…I kept going. Each and every week, we put out a new show and at this point we are over 5 years strong.

The goal of the show was to create content that provided value to the audience. I never tried to sell anything. I didn't really even mention my company. To put it simply, I gave first.

And that, my friends, is why I am writing this book today.

The goal of this book is to show you some ideas that you can put into play in your business right away . Some of them will seem simple (and they are). Some of them will make you uncomfortable. But all of them are ideas that I have put to work in my business in one way or another to set my team apart.

So, if you are a salesperson, entrepreneur, leader or person that just wants to stand out, I hope this book is for you.

Now let's get started so you can create Success in the *Give First Economy*.

CHAPTER 1

WE ARE IN A GIVE FIRST ECONOMY!

> "The person that gives the value first has the leverage."
> *Gary Vaynerchuk*

I first mentioned the *Give First Economy* in my book, *Delivering Marketing Joy*, many years ago. It's funny, because though at the time, it was something that many people commented on, it was not a fully formed concept for me. Since then I've spoken about it at events, written about it in blogs, and talked about it in podcasts and in videos. And what I know is, it's even more true today than when I first typed it years ago.

We are in a *Give First Economy*.

In this book, I want to talk about what that means, how to understand it, what to do about, and tactics to succeed in this new world.

To explain what a *Give First Economy* is, let's start with what it is not.

The *Give First Economy* is not the "good old boys" club. It is not about a Country Club mentality or just doing business with the people you play golf with. It's not about favors and scratching backs in order to win favor. That sort of old school networking has certainly worked in the past, whether you like it or not. But it is not what I am talking about. And I don't think it's a path for long term success in today's culture.

So...what is the *Give First Economy*?

First and foremost, it's about value. It's about providing more than you are paid for. It's about doing business "the right way". Simply put, I believe that the person, salesperson, entrepreneur or company that has the strength to provide value first, will win...long term.

Marketing Has Changed from Push to Pull

Why are we now in the *Give First Economy*? Because times have changed! Since the beginning of marketing and advertising, we have lived in a "push" world. If you wanted to succeed and for people to know you, you had to push out your message. You needed to be loud and aggressive. The company that pushed their message out the strongest and the loudest won. These companies had the money and influence to create ads on every TV, they reached every person through radio and they could even purchase Super Bowl Ads. They pushed and pushed until they won.

But with the onset of the internet (and social media) that has changed. Consumers have the ability to tune us out. They have the ability to shut us off. You, as a customer, have the ability to follow my business or unfollow. You can block me. And, maybe more importantly, when the transaction goes wrong, the customer has the ability to tell other customers all about it. The customer has a voice…and a loud one.

The power in the relationship has changed.

We need to PULL customers in. We need to provide value. We need to help to educate them and entertain them. We need to build trust and show integrity, before they even have a chance to purchase our product.

We need to "give first."

It's Great News

And here's the thing. As a consumer, this is a great thing! We often look at these shifts in the marketplace and see them as an inconvenience. The rules are changing, and as entrepreneurs and marketers, we don't always like that. We have to re-think what we are doing and what is working. I get that.

But when we look at many of these changes from the customers' point of view, they are great. These changes are rewarding (and will continue to reward) those businesses and organizations that do things the "right way". It can make a very large world small again.

The example I use when I give talks around the country has to do with your grandma (yes, yours). Back when your grandmother went to the store, the butcher probably knew her by name. He knew her kids' names and what she liked to cook on a Friday night. He might have even known what your grandfather's favorite cut of meat was. He took great care of her, not only because she was a customer, but in a small town she had influence. If he took good care of her, she might tell her friends. And if he did not take great care of her, she most certainly would tell her friends. He provided great service because it was good business.

The *Give First Economy* rewards companies that do this today. The customer has value and influence and should be treated with respect. Now, the culture and the economy are rewarding <u>them</u> financially.

As we go through this book, I am going to outline examples of businesses, entrepreneurs, artists and sales professionals who are doing just that. They are creating value for prospects. They are building an audience. They are gaining attention so that when they have a new product, they have a built-in audience to sell it to. And when there is a mistake (and there are always going to be mistakes) they have built up the credibility and trust to weather the storm.

My goal is to give you some tactics so you can do the same thing. In each chapter we will discuss tactics and examples of how you and your organization can stand out in a crowded marketplace by giving first.

But first…meet *Gary Vaynerchuk*.

GIVING FIRST WITH GARY VAYNERCHUK

If you want a case study about how to succeed in the *Give First Economy*, look no further than Gary Vaynerchuk. "GaryVee" is a living embodiment of this concept and he has been doing it for years! For those who don't know about Vaynerchuk, let me give you the very basics (but I dare you to spend 5 minutes looking him up. You will be buried in amazing content that will keep you busy for weeks).

The short story goes like this. After working in his family's liquor store for years as a kid, Gary came back from college and took over the family business. He took the business from a $3 Million operation to a $60 Million business in just 5 years. He did so by using both traditional marketing, email marketing (which was still new at the time), and Google AdWords. Then, in 2008, Gary Vaynerchuk took to YouTube to create WineLibraryTV.

This is where the "Give First" magic began. Gary was a study in both consistency and authenticity. Believe it or not, there are over 1000 episodes of WineLibraryTV! That is not a typo. Gary and his team created over 1000 episodes of an online show about wine. Remember that when you're frustrated after creating a week of blog posts with limited response! He just kept producing!

And my favorite part? Gary panned about two thirds of the wine he reviewed.

Yep. He went on a show that he produced and paid for and told his audience NOT to buy that wine from him (or anyone else)! But that's the magic. Just think what happened when he told you to <u>buy</u> a wine! He had built up so much credibility, that his recommendation carried so much more weight!

When Gary left the family wine business to start VaynerMedia (digital media agency), he did it again. He started a web show answering questions about business, marketing, social media and more called the "AskGaryVee" show. Vaynerchuk continues to create new and innovative content with the full idea of providing value up front. He is a marvel in how to "Succeed in the Give First Economy."

Oh, and as an interesting aside (at least to me), as I am writing this, Gary has decided to get back into the Wine Business. He is using his abilities and (almost as importantly) his audience to launch the new company Empathy Wines. You can find information at Empathywines.com.

CHAPTER 2

GIVE OUT JOY

"Life is an echo. What you put out you get back.
What you give you get."
Zig Ziglar

You made it through Chapter 1. "Okay," you might be thinking, "I believe you. I need to give first. But what does that mean? What are some things I can start doing right away to stand out in this climate?"

Great question.

My goal is to dig into some real things you can start to do today in order to impact your business, your organization or your personal brand. These techniques work. They are actionable. And hopefully, they are a bit inspiring!

But be forewarned, these are going to seem like common sense. They will seem simple. But here is a very important secret: simple is not the same as easy. There are so many things in life that are easy to diagnose. But just because they are simple to point out, does not mean they are easy to execute. That's why it's always easy to tell people what THEY should do to fix their issues. Solutions are often simple...not easy.

That's why this is one of my favorite quotes in the world:

"The greatest distance in the world is
the distance between "I know" and "I do."

When I talk about these principles, I always like to take some time here. That's because at some point during this journey, you will inevitably say, "Yeah...I know that." I know you do. The problem is most of us are not executing on these principles... at least not consistently enough.

The reason I know this quote is true is because I KNOW, without a doubt, how to have 6 pack abs. I know how to be more fit. We all do. I need to eat better quality food, work out more and drink less beer.

I know how to do it. I just don't (consistently) do it. So, when you catch yourself saying "I know," just take a moment. Ask yourself this series of questions:

"Yes, I know this concept...but am I doing it?"

"Could I do it more?"

"Am I doing it consistently?"

"Can I up my game?"

When you stop and ask these questions, my guess is it will get you back on track.

Now...let's dig into the power of giving out Joy!

Give Out Joy

Some days it feels like the world is drowning in negativity. Studies will tell you that 89% of what you see every day is negative. Whether it is through the media, social media or even in the 3D world, everyone seems to be frustrated or complaining.

And don't just blame the media. That's lazy. The fact is most days CNN is not who is filling up my Facebook feed with complaining. It's us. It's you. Don't get me wrong, the media helps fuel this fire, but they are not the only ones throwing logs on it. We all have a share of the blame.

The great thing about social media is that everyone has a voice. The bad thing is...everyone has a voice. As you turn on your device, it seems half the people posting are snarky trolls and the other half create a new reason to play the victim every day. Negativity is all around us.

Once we understand that, the question is obvious. What do we do about it?

The answer is simple (but not always easy) ...Give Out Joy.

In a world where nearly 90% of what we see is negative, most people are hungering for something different. We are looking for someone to shine a light on good things. We are looking for inspiration. And the reality is, when you push out good and joy into the world, we stand out in a crowded marketing place.

When we are creating a business, an organization or a personal brand, we are always trying to prove to the marketplace we are better. But as Mike Michalowicz says (author of *Profit First*, *Pumpkin Plan*, and many other great business books),

"In the minds of our customers, better is not better. Different is better."

The fact is, when seemingly everything we see in the world is negative, a positive person (or brand) can be a shining light. It stands out. So, by giving out joy, creating joy and spreading joy, you start to stand out in the marketplace.

Now you might be thinking, "Great. But I am already a positive person!". My guess is, you are not as positive as you think (sorry to be negative). The fact is, as humans, we are not great at self-auditing. That's why surveys will tell you that MOST people think they are an above average driver. The math tells you that's not true.

So how do we know if we are positive or negative?

Let's start with a simple exercise.

This is something I have done in sessions that I give all over the U.S. I start with a simple question.

Then I follow up with another simple question.

"How many of you ARE that person?"

Silence. No hands. People start to look around the room and small uncomfortable laughs start as they realize the joke.

Then the punchline comes as I say, "I have given this talk all over the country and I have never met the one jerk that is filling up all of our Facebook feeds!".

No one thinks it's them. As I said, we are not great at self-auditing. We don't think we are being negative. We think we "are just venting". We might even think we are being funny. But we generally don't think we could possibly be perceived as a negative person.

Let's go to the tape!

Go to your Facebook feed (or your social media outlet of choice) and look at the last 10 posts. Be introspective. Think about how they might be looked at from the outside world. Now, if 4 or more of those posts could be perceived as negative (and that's not up to you, right?), you are likely thought of as a negative person by many of the people that follow you.

Oh…and here's the caveat. Political posts and religious posts can be viewed as negative.

We all have that "crazy uncle" that posts on their favorite social media platform about 9 times a day outlining why the current U.S. President is a criminal. Sure…those people are easy to spot. But what about you? What do your posts look like?

The push back I sometimes get when I am speaking has to do with "religious" posts. What do I mean by that? I am not suggesting you should not celebrate your faith. I am suggesting that tone matters. Consider it.

On the other hand, you really should be authentic. You should not just change your personality to fit what people want. I don't think you should, and I am not suggesting that. If you WANT to post political rants, that's your call. What I AM saying is you should be intentional. Most people just sort of randomly post and share without any real thought as to how they are perceived by the outside world.

I do think you should be intentional about it. And, if you want to stand out and make a difference and create a personal brand that people want to follow in the *Give First Economy*, I think you should consider intentionally being joyful.

Where to Start

If you like the idea of pushing out more joy but are wondering where to start, here are a few ideas. Use these as a jumping off point and run with it!

Share Joyful News: This doesn't have to just be about the highlight reel of your life. Seek out good things in your community and share them! Look for good things in your organization or relationships and give them a shout out! It will not only be a great and joyful noise coming from you, but it will make them feel good too!

Create Uplifting Content: If you are so inclined, write blogs that help to uplift. Create Instagram posts designed to admire. Put together a video where you interview people doing good in your industry. Shining a light on the good in the world can always be a great place to start.

Give Compliments: We will talk more about this in the next chapter but make it a point to give people praise.

Smile: Want a funny exercise? The next time you drop your kid off at school (or drive to any public place), take the time to look at the faces of the other drivers. Wow. You will see a LOT of grumpy faces! Take the time to give people your smile. It's funny...you will see people give it back.

In the next chapter, we will dig into how you can stand out by giving out more Praise and Thanks. You are about to make a lot of people feel better!

But first, let's meet *Casey Neistat!*

GIVING FIRST WITH CASEY NEISTAT

Casey Neistat is one of the world's most famous vloggers. Casey creates a daily vlog that provides entertainment, advice, and inspiration for millions on YouTube. And when I say, "for millions", that is not an exaggeration. As a matter of fact, with over 10 million subscribers to his channel, I am probably underselling his influence.

Casey is well known for his high-quality videos and his creativity in the story telling style of vlogging. As a matter of fact, I believe he is one of the true pioneers that made the art more mainstream.

One of Neistat's more famous (or infamous) videos came when he got a ticket in New York City for not riding his bike in the bike lane. His problem with the ticket, as he tried to explain, is that there are often things IN the bike lane. So, it's actually safer for everyone (especially the biker) if they don't ride there. Instead of just complaining, Casey made a video. He shot video of himself riding in the bike lane and repeatedly running into things that are in the way...sending him crashing off his bike. Spoiler alert: the video ends with him riding in the bike lane and running into his final obstacle...a police car. (At the time I am writing this, this video has nearly 22 Million views!)

Neistat started a daily vlog several years ago. That's right. Casey, in addition to a family and other business interests, created a high quality, fun and creative video on his YouTube channel...every day. Sometimes he would create an inspirational video (giving). Sometimes he would review new technology (providing value).

And sometimes the videos would show his travel adventures. In each video, Casey gave insight into his opinions, his personality and his life.

Casey is a true pioneer in the *Give First Economy*. Want to learn more? Head to YouTube and search Casey.

GIVE THANKS AND PRAISE

"Saying thank you is more than good manners.
It's good spirituality."
Alfred Agache.

This chapter is the mother of all "I know" and "I do" activity. So, let's start with mothers (and fathers).

When it comes to good parents, as your child begins to talk, what are the first couple of phrases you teach them? Say it with me, "Please and thank you". Great! It's no surprise to me that the people reading this book are either good parents or were raised by them! That's right! Please and thank you.

But here's a secret most people won't tell you. As parents, we get tired of hearing "please".

Please can I stay up later?

Please can I go to my friends?

Please can I have one more?

Please? Please? Please?

It's exhausting.

But you know what you (or your mother) never tires of hearing? You guessed it. Thank you. That simple sign of appreciation is much rarer. And even if it's not, it's never annoying. We appreciate the appreciation.

Guess what? Your customers are exactly the same. They are hearing "please" from you, your competitors, their employees and the whole world all day long, 365 days a year. It's exhausting for them, too.

Give Thanks!

What they don't hear enough is "thank you."

How often do you really spend time saying, "thank you"? Not just the basic "hey thanks" you say in passing or the automatic email that says, "thanks for your purchase". Those are fine...I guess. But they don't take effort and are not really sincere. How often do you stop by a customer's office just to thank them for their business? How often do you pick up the phone to do the same? How often do you schedule a meeting with a person in your organization just to take the time to applaud their efforts?

> In almost all organizations,
> there is an Appreciation Gap.
>
> Let's look at one of the scariest
> and most exciting statistics in business.
>
> 69% of customers who leave you,
> will do so because of perceived indifference.

In other words, nearly 7 out of 10 of the customers who walk away from you or your business, will do so because they don't think you care. Seriously? That number freaks me out...and it should you too.

On the other hand, it's exciting. Why? Because, quite frankly, it's easy to fix.

We fix it by showing appreciation. Real appreciation. We don't just assume "they know". We make it a point and a mission to really let people know how much they mean to us. Here are a couple of easy ways to make sure your best customers (and employees) know you really do appreciate them.

Just "Thanks:" Go to your clients or your employees with a simple "thanks meeting." If it's a client, let them know you are only there to say, "thank you for their business". In other words, it's not a sandwich of "thanks" but also a sales call. If they say they want to purchase something, great. But too many times we ACT as if we want to say "thanks," but it's really disguised as a sales call. That's not appreciation; it's a tactic. Your prospects and customers will sniff that out immediately and you might do more harm than good. At the very least, they won't feel appreciated. If it's an employee schedule a quick meeting. Both will probably give you quizzical looks because they are not used to this sort of meeting, but both will appreciate it.

Send a Card: Yes...we are going old school. Take the time and send out a simple greeting card showing your appreciation. It's simple. But think about where you open your mail. Most people, when I ask that, tell me they sort through their mail over the trash can. So, when you get a nice, sincere, thoughtful card of thanks, it not only means a lot, it also really stands out.

Oh, and don't just take my word for it, in a recent article in *Reuters*, job seekers are finding value in Thank You notes (yes, we are all in sales in some way).

> **To some it may seem laughably archaic to hand-write a note, drop it in snail mail and hope the recipient gets it a few days later. One study by staffing firm Accountemps, found that only 24 percent of job applicants bother to send thank-you notes these days.**

> **But here is the rub: 80 percent of human resources managers surveyed felt those messages were useful in evaluating potential hires.**

In addition, studies show that people who send out regular thank you notes show fewer signs of anxiety and depression. It's time to embrace the Thank You note.

Appreciation Program: This is for your best clients. Most businesses have a rule that 80% of the revenue comes from 20% of the clients. This is for that 20%. Create a quarterly program where you get a simple gift for your best clients...just to say "thanks."

About every 3 months, you get a group of gifts that you can either send out or hand deliver to your cream of the crop customers. These are the ones that you REALLY want to keep. You want to make sure they know you appreciate them!

This is a simple but effective way to show up differently for your best customers. It also systematizes the process, so you don't forget. You're busy (especially if you have great customers). It's easy to let this recognition get away from you. The fact is, that's why most people and organizations, don't say thank you often enough. They want to. They might even mean to. But it gets away from them. By creating a program and a process, you make it a priority and it gets done.

Whatever you decide to do, just make sure you make it a priority to stop saying "please" so much and to start saying "thank you" more often.

Giving Praise

A kissing cousin of appreciation is praise. If you want to stand out in the *Give First Economy* (and if you've come this far, we can assume you do), then shelling out sincere praise is a great way to do it.

In most organizations, communities, or wherever you operate, there are good people doing good work. Maybe you're one of them! And if you are, you know that much of the good work that is being done is, unfortunately, largely unappreciated.

If you want to earn a special place in a person's heart, take notice of their good contribution. Take some time and sincerely give them praise and thanks for their good work. Consistently doing this in a sincere way, will make people love you.

Is the Chamber Director doing a great job improving your community? Let them know.

Is the marketing director in your company creating amazing new sales material? Call it out!

Maybe someone in your town keeps their flowers beautifully and it makes the community better. Take the time to make a big deal about it.

As Billy Joel said, "Tell them about it!"

Now let's meet marketing legend, Seth Godin.

GIVING FIRST WITH SETH GODIN

There is a difference between Heroes and Mentors. A mentor is someone who you have a consistent relationship with and helps you grow into the person you want to be. A hero is someone you admire from afar and helps to inspire you to do better and grow. In the *Give First Economy*, there can actually be overlap in these two areas.

Seth Godin is proof of that for me.

There is no question that Seth is a marketing hero for me. I like to say that he is the Godfather of modern marketing. He is the author of 17 best-selling books. He's an entrepreneur. He is an independent thinker. He has taken on topics ranging from marketing to education and has even created an alternative to higher education in the real world called "AltMBA."

One of the ways that Seth shows up is through his blog. He "gives first" by creating a blog every single day. Some of his blogs are long though often the posts are short and sweet. But day in and day out, Godin shows up for his audience and gives his thoughts generously. In doing so, he has created one of the most read blogs in the world. He has done so, as he has pointed out in his amazing podcast, *Akimbo*, while never writing the number one post of the day. Instead, he has become one of the most respected voices in marketing by <u>showing up</u> every single day.

One of the highlights of my content journey gave me an opportunity to interview Seth. It happened not long after I started *Delivering Marketing Joy* (my weekly web show). I had recorded around 20 episodes when I had the chance to interview Godin on a podcast with my friend, Mark Graham. Mark had set up the interview and we were going to live stream it. I could not have been more excited!

Just before we went live, Seth told me that he had seen my new show. I couldn't believe it. He even went into some detail about one of the interviews (so I knew he actually HAD seen it). Then he said something that stopped me. "I like what you are doing. Keep it up. In three years, you will be glad you did." he said.

At that moment, I was questioning whether I should keep going. In that one statement, Seth answered that question and inspired me to keep it up. For episode #100, Seth agreed to join me as a guest on the show! To me, it was the ultimate pay off to nearly 2 years of hard work.

Seth Godin is not only a hero to me...he is a mentor too. He is a best-selling author, entrepreneur, podcaster and giver.

He gives first...and millions of his fans are grateful for it.

CHAPTER 4

GIVE EXPECTING NOTHING IN RETURN

> "There can be no greater gift than that of giving one's time and energy to help others without expecting anything in return."
> Nelson Mandela

When I am speaking on this topic, this is the time of the presentation when I ask the audience if they have ever heard of the "Rule of Reciprocity." Whether you have heard the term or not, you know what it means. Nearly every culture has been built on the idea.

The term, the "Rule of Reciprocity" comes from the book *Influence*, by Dr. Robert Caldini. (As a side note, this a must-read book for anyone in marketing and sales). The rule of reciprocity, in its most basic form, is simple. If someone gives you something, you feel naturally compelled to do something for them in return. If you welcome your new neighbor with a welcome basket, they will often feel compelled to give you a bottle of wine "as a thank you."

It's basic. It's simple. And in the purest form, it's beautiful.

The problem is, as Gary Vaynerchuk said, "Marketers ruin everything!" Over time, people have come to understand this rule and have used it to manipulate people to doing things they don't want to do. They have used the rule of reciprocity like a hammer to beat people into a guilty state when they feel required to "give back."

Most of us have probably felt this in one form or another at some point in our life.

That means, as humans, we have a really strong bullshit detector for people who want to "give" us something. We don't trust it and we don't believe it. We have seen people manipulate us or others and so we are very skeptical that someone would want to provide us value without gaining anything in return.

That's why, if we want to succeed in the *Give First Economy*, we must Give Value while expecting nothing in return. This takes the value of this concept up a few notches in a very real way.

It works for a couple of reasons.

They Will Sniff You Out

As I mentioned above, our customers and prospects have developed a sense of when someone is trying to take advantage of them. They have done this, for the most part, by assuming that everyone that is providing something that is "too good to be true" is trying to trick them. So, if you are just trying to manipulate people into doing business with you, they will likely sniff you out right away.

And even if they don't, they will after the first transaction. Remember, no successful business was ever created from one sale. When people manipulate this rule, it's so they can get a short-term sale. They are not worried about a long-term relationship. But as I mentioned in an earlier chapter, that is a problem in a world where every customer has a real and powerful voice.

I tell my team at Hasseman Marketing that I want to create "20-year customers." That puts us in the right mindset of trying to create value that will last a lifetime. If not, the customer has the power to find someone who will.

Great news, though – if you're not just focused on taking advantage of them, something magical happens.

They Will Be Delightfully Surprised

The bad news is, we have been conditioned to believe that people are not out to give first. This is why we have sayings like,

"Too good to be true."

"Nothing in life is free."

The good news is, when your prospects and customers come to understand that you are the real deal, they will be blown away! This is where the *Give First Economy* really gets momentum.

You see, Intent is the real superpower.

When your intent is to provide real value and create real relationships, that is exactly what you'll get. You will find customers that trust your advice, forgive your mistakes and value your relationship. The great irony is that when you give and expect nothing in return, your return is much greater.

Giving Is Hard...Do It Anyway

It's usually about now in the conversation when the "Yeah, buts" arrive. The "yeah, buts" come in many forms, but they all come down to one basic question.

"If I provide all of this value up front, won't I get taken advantage of?"

Let's keep this short and sweet. Yes. You will.

When you provide value to people in advance, there will be some people that will take advantage of you.

Let me tell you a story.

I got a phone call from a family member. She was in a relationship that she was trying to get out of. She had lined up an apartment. She had a job. But the one thing that that was keeping her from leaving was having a car in her own name. She needed transportation in order to move on. She was at the dealership and had picked out a car.

The problem was her credit wasn't great. She needed someone to co-sign the loan for her to get the car. She needed my help.

Without hesitation, I said of course. I wanted to help her, and I understood that having some basic transportation could give her the independence she wanted and needed. I was proud that I could help.

And that, of course, is when it went sideways.

First, I started getting letters in the mail from the bank. These late notices let me know that the payments weren't being made on time. In the short term, I talked to her and she would make the payments (albeit late). This went on for several months.

Then she left town...and took the car with her.

When the letters from the bank kept coming, I had to start paying for a car that I did not own and didn't even know where it was! Then the car showed back up in my town. I called my lawyer and told him that I was going to go get the car. That's when he dropped the bomb on me.

"You can't," he said. "The car is not in your name. If you take the car it will be Grand Theft Auto!"

Long story short, I gave first with the best of intentions...and I got taken advantage of.

After this very frustrating situation, it would have been easy to say, "never again." To be honest, that was my attitude for about a week. But then I came to realize, that it's not that I cannot ever help someone again. I just need to learn my lesson so I can be smarter the next time I help in this way.

When it comes to building your business, you might run into a situation like this. As a matter of fact, you probably will. But remember that you are thinking long term...right? You want to create 20-year customers that you will have a relationship with for the long term.

If, for example, you provide samples, plans, and creative to a prospect and they take your information and shop you out with it, it hurts in the short term. But in the long term, they have shown you what kind of customer they will be. These are not the kind of prospects that deserve your services long term.

Will you be pissed in the short term? You bet. But when you change the way you look at this situation, it changes your perspective on creating a Give First Business.

CHAPTER 5

GIVE MORE THAN THEY PAY FOR

> "Give people more than they expect
> and do it cheerfully."
> Tony Robbins

When it comes to succeeding in the *Give First Economy*, you will spend a lot of time providing value upfront. As we have discussed, doing so will create a relationship of trust with your prospects and turn them into customers.

But what happens when they finally decide to "buy?" Do you get to coast now? Of course not. Now is when you get to prove to your prospect (and now customer) that you are all you have promised.

Of course, you need to provide the product or service on time and on budget. The fact is, in many cases, this is enough. By doing so, you will show that you are an organization that honors your commitments. You take care of the customer. You deliver. That's good.

Standing out in today's "gotta have it now, Amazon will deliver, Alexa will listen, I blink my eyes twice and it's here" culture takes more. As my buddy, Bill Petrie (President of PromoCorner) says, "if you deliver your project on time and on budget, that's great. But everyone is doing that! That is the basement. That is the expectation."

It's fine. But it's not remarkable. You need remarkable.

There are many ways to be remarkable, but many (if not most) of them cost a lot of money, time, manpower and more. They're hard to execute, even once. And they are nearly impossible to do time and time again.

That is why I love the concept of G.L.U.E.

Giving

Little

Unexpected

Extras

This concept comes from my friend, Stan Phelps, from his book, *The Purple Goldfish*. In the *Purple Goldfish*, Stan explains that some of the best companies in the world are creating differentiation from adding value in the transaction.

While at its core, this makes sense from the customers' perspective (I mean who doesn't want to get more, right?). Let's dig into the G.L.U.E. concept a bit here.

Giving: This is the basis for the whole book, but I think it makes sense to spend just a moment on this. Giving means providing something (anything) of value for the customer. If it means something to you, but not the customer, that's not the idea. Even in this stage, after the transaction, it's about providing value that they will appreciate.

Little: Here's the thing. It does NOT have to be huge. It can be a little gesture. What we know in business and in life (and is the whole point behind the book, *Purple Goldfish*) is that little things often make a BIG difference. These little gestures show that you care. It might be an extra product that they did not pay for, or a handwritten thank you note from the CEO. These "little things" can often make an organization truly stand out.

Unexpected: I think this is key. The best gestures are often unexpected. That's what makes them special. If you do something "extra" every single time, then it's not extra. It creates a new expectation in the customer and, eventually, does not delight. As a matter of fact, if you don't do this gesture in the future, you let the customer down. That's why it's tough to systematize these efforts. They have to be personal (or at least appear to be) to work.

Extra: The final component is that the gesture must be above and beyond the transaction. As I said earlier, doing the transaction "right" is the baseline. That is fine...but it does not delight. The G.L.U.E. concept surprises and delights because of that little extra.

CD BABY Jet Email

One of my favorite examples of G.L.U.E. in action comes from the founder of CD Baby, Derek Sivers. Sivers created CD Baby to feature independent musicians and their work. They were an early online company, and Derek and his team did a lot to innovate in this space.

One of them was a simple, yet over the top, email response.

Sivers tells the story that he was working on the website and had created an auto responder that let the customer know that they had received their order. But, as he thought about it, that "thanks for your order" email just did not seem like enough. He wanted to something more. He wanted something fun and personal. So, he went to work… and created a masterpiece.

When you went to the CD Baby website and hit the "buy" button, you got THIS email:

Your CD has been gently taken from our CD Baby shelves with sterilized contamination-free gloves and placed onto a satin pillow.

A team of 50 employees inspected your CD and polished it to make sure it was in the best possible condition before mailing.

Our packing specialist from Japan lit a candle and a hush fell over the crowd as he put your CD into the finest gold-lined box that money can buy.

We all had a wonderful celebration afterwards and the whole party marched down the street to the post office where the entire town of Portland waved "Bon Voyage!" to your package, on its way to you, in our private CD Baby jet on this day, Friday, June 6th.

I hope you had a wonderful time shopping at CD Baby. We sure did. Your picture is on our wall as "Customer of the Year." We're all exhausted but can't wait for you to come back to CDBABY.COM!!

This email was sent out with every order that went out from CD Baby. If you google "CD Baby Jet" you will find hundreds of thousands of responses. What an impact! That is sticky. That is G.L.U.E.

Giving: Yes, this has value. The customer wanted to know their order had been received and shipped. Check.

Little: It cost exactly nothing. They did not send out extra product. They sent out joy.

Unexpected: I mean, who would expect this email? This is fun and over the top and amazing.

Extra: Finally, it is extra. They could have sent the standard "your order has shipped" email and that would have been fine. It would not, however, have been remarkable.

What does this look like for you and your organization? How can you make a small gesture that can help you show up differently to your customers or prospects? Now is a great time to consider doing it. Here are a few random samples to get your wheels turning.

Auto Shop: If you offer oil changes, have your team, select one or two random cars and put a gift certificate for a free coffee at a local coffee shop. It brightens the customer's day and gives some business to a fellow entrepreneur.

Bakery: This one is obvious, right? Add one donut to an order between a designated time on the clock.

Retail: Instead of making everyone sign up for our "VIP list" for special treatment, give a random 10% off to customers or give them a free coffee while they shop. That little extra will surprise and delight... and it might make them stay in the store longer!

You get the idea. Start looking around your organization for ways where you can lift your service above the bare minimum. You will find ways to create the very best kind of "shock and awe" in the eyes of your customers.

Now let's meet *John Lee Dumas!*

GIVING FIRST WITH JOHN LEE DUMAS

At this point, many people know John Lee Dumas (or JLD) as the leader of Fire Nation and the owner and founder of Entrepreneur on Fire. He is one of the most recognizable podcasters in the world and has the chance to interview the most famous entrepreneurs all over the world.

But when he started out, he was just struggling to find his place (like a lot of us). Dumas had served in the Armed Forces and came back to find that his office job did not excite him. He tried a few things and was working hard in real estate in California. While doing this job, he was constantly looking for things to inspire him and keep him motivated.

One of his friends turned him on to podcasts and he was hooked. He burned through all the podcasts on the market and was looking for more when he realized something important, no one was doing this every day. He would listen to an episode but then have to wait a week or a month for another one to come out. He needed more and he figured other people were just like him.

So JLD set out to fill that void...and fill it he did! Dumas posted a new podcast with an interview every day for 2000 days in a row! Every single day, John showed up, building a rabid and faithful audience (and fan base) all the while.

Now he has a successful speaking career, business and still has a great interview podcast. But he got started by showing up every day to provide value to an audience...and by Giving First.

CHAPTER 6

GIVE VALUE THROUGH SOCIAL MEDIA AND CONTENT

"We need to stop interrupting what people are interested in, and BE what people are interested in."
David Beebe

One of the most powerful tools to leverage in the *Give First Economy* is Social Media and Content Marketing.

If you are a headline reader, you hear all the time how social media is going to be the end of civilization as we know it. I think we all need to pump the brakes on this. Social media (and a phone in general) is a tool. The challenge for many people is, they are letting these tools rule their lives. That is an important topic...but that's another book!

What I can tell you is that to truly succeed and thrive in today's *Give First Economy*, you need to leverage these tools.

It has long been said that "People buy from people they like, know and trust." Though I believe there was some thought, as the internet came into existence, that this might go away; it has not. In some ways, it's grown stronger. Using social media and content marketing, you allow people to "like, know and trust" you (and your organization) at scale.

Now here's the thing. This is not strictly a social media and content marketing book. There are plenty of those. Great ones actually...and I will give you a few that I recommend at the end of this chapter. If you want to dig deeper in this topic (and I think you should) there are great books on tactics from Guy Kawasaki, Joe Puliizi, Gary Vaynerchuk and more.

But in this book, I want to give you a 10,000-foot view of how to get started (or get better) on your content strategy.

It's NOT For You

The problem I see with most content and social media strategies is simple. They're creating their content based on what is important to the company...not the customer. Great content is NOT an ad. No one spends time looking for new advertising to consume. The best content is information that helps the customer answer a question or solve a problem for them...not for you.

Remember...it's about Giving First.

If you're not sure where to start, think back to your conversations with customers and prospects. As you talk to them, you are sure to be asked questions about your products or services. Often, you get asked the same five to ten questions over and over again. Take a few minutes to think of those questions and how you answer them.

Those answers can become the foundation for your new content. By answering these questions, you are creating value. You are giving.

Again, it's not about selling. It's about creating real information for the customer.

How do you decide what kind of content to create? Think about your strengths and what you like best.

Are you a person that likes to talk? Then you might create a short video answering each question. You can post those to YouTube and your website.

Would you rather write? Then your best bet might be to create a blog where you can write out the question and then give your answer in written form.

Maybe you love to take pictures! Going straight to Facebook or Instagram to showcase the solution to a problem could be perfect.

The idea is simple: When creating content, play to your strengths.

4 C's of Content

Once you have decided on the vehicle or platform where you will create your content, you might be wondering where to start. My good buddy, Bill Petrie and I created a rule called the 4 C's of Content that can help you know if you are on the right track.

The 4 C's of Content stand for **Creative**, **Consumable**, **Consistent**... and **Courage**. Let's dig into each of these here.

Creative: Being creative has always been the hardest thing to define in this list. I mean, what does "creative" mean? And, if you are a person that does not see themselves as "a creative person," should you just give up now? In a word, no. I think of creative (in this context) as customer centric. You don't have to be Mark Twain. What you do need to do is think of the topic you are trying to discuss, or the question you are trying to answer, from the customer's perspective.

Why are they struggling with this?

What don't they understand?

Why are they frustrated?

Now, answer the question FOR them! By solving a problem in the customer's eyes (whether they buy from you or not), you will be creative.

Consumable: This one often makes people feel better. When you start out creating content, you don't need to write a 10,000-word blog post. Your videos don't need to be an hour. As a matter of fact, they should not be. You want to create things that are consumable. Make your content long enough to answer the question…and then stop. Ask yourself this question, "how many times in the last month have you decided whether to watch a video based on how long it was?" When I ask this question to groups, nearly everyone raises their hand. If you are doing this as a consumer of content, then so are your customers and prospects. Create content that is short and sweet and consumable!

Consistent: This is probably my biggest pet peeve when it comes to content. That's because it's the thing most people (including myself) struggle with. If you want to build an audience, you need to be consistent with your content. We have all seen the opposite. You go to an organization's Facebook page and you see a bunch of content from 6 months ago…and then it stops. It's like someone in the organization went to a seminar and decided "I am going to go all in on social media." They got after it for 3 weeks, then the whirlwind got in the way.

I get it. Creating content on a regular basis is hard work. But if you want to create value and, as Seth Godin would say, build a tribe, you need to be consistent with your content. If you think of nearly all the most influential content creators, they have built an audience by being consistent.

Seth Godin blogs every day.

Casey Neistat created a vlog every day.

Jeff Haden wrote an article on Inc.com every day.

Gary Vaynerchuk started a wine show on YouTube that aired every day.

John Lee Dumas built an audience by podcasting every day.

But here's the good news...you get to choose how often. Though the folks above created content every day, that does not mean you have to. You can create your content twice a week, once a week or once a month. You just have to be consistent about it.

Bill Petrie, who I have talked about several times in this book, created a great audience with his blog by writing it once a week. He puts out a blog every Monday. But here's the thing, it comes out EVERY Monday. If the office is closed, his blog comes out. If it's Christmas, his blog comes out. No matter what, his blog comes out once a week, every week.

He is consistent.

Courage: This is the "C" that I rarely hear people address, when it comes to content. The fact is it takes courage to put yourself out there.

Whether you want to create a blog post or a company, a video or a presentation, we all have to overcome the same thing. "That voice."

It's the voice that's in each of our heads that tells us that we are "not good enough" or "not smart enough" or that "no one will care." We have all heard that inner voice that asks, "why would anyone care what you have to say?" Or even the one that tells us "this will make you look stupid."

In addition, I think we look at people who regularly put out content, or start businesses, or speak in public and think "they must not have that voice in their head." They must be so confident. They're not insecure. It must be easy for them.

**Here is a good news/bad news moment.
They have that voice, too. We all have that voice.**

I hope this is good news for you. If you're thinking of putting yourself out there, you are not alone. We all have that voice to overcome. Every time I post a blog, or a video, or get ready to make a sales call, I have the voice that tells me I am about to make a mistake. But here's the thing...I do it anyway.

It just takes Courage.

**You need to have the
Courage to Consistently Create Consumable Content.**

Give Engagement

If then, as I just said, everyone has "that voice" then it stands to reason that your customers and prospects have that voice, too. They too, are wondering if anyone cares. They'll be struggling with the idea that they may come off as stupid.

That is why engagement can be such a powerful tool in the *Give First Economy*.

When your customer or prospect posts a blog or a video or any other piece of content, you have the ability to support them with likes, comments or shares. Obviously, you want to be thoughtful. But it's a great and simple way for you to show your support.

Gary Vaynerchuk calls this "The Power of the Wink."

Vaynerchuk tells the story of when he had the opportunity to go to a baseball game in New York when he was a young child. Rickey Henderson, playing for the Oakland A's at the time, was playing. At the end of one inning, Henderson was running off the field and looked at young Vaynerchuk and winked.

Bing! Gary was a huge Rickey Henderson fan for life! Why? Because Henderson took just a moment to create a human connection that let Gary know he mattered. It's simple and it's powerful...and it's the power of the wink.

You can create this sort of connection when you thoughtfully engage with your customer's content. It will take some time to do this right. But if you are willing to invest this time, you will be surprised with the power of the connections you can create.

As my friend, Danny Rosin once told me, "Social media will never replace the handshake. But it can turn a handshake into a hug."

I have seen this happen. It comes from creating value. It comes from pushing out good. It comes with creating a real human relationship with the Power of the Wink.

Now let me introduce you to Jeff Haden.

GIVING FIRST WITH JEFF HADEN

When Jeff Haden started his journey on "giving first" he was a ghostwriter. And although he had had some success, how could he prove it? I mean, he was a ghostwriter! Part of the deal with being a great ghostwriter is you cannot tell anyone that you were actually the writer! You sign iron clad contracts to make sure that doesn't happen.

Understandable, sure. But how you show people that you have great writing chops, when you can't show them what you have written?

So, Jeff decided to choose himself.

He took the opportunity to write for Inc.com. Though he could have been paid a flat fee by the article, Haden decided to go another way. He was not doing this for the money, so he decided to focus on providing as much value as he could so he could build a real audience.

Haden committed to writing an article on Inc.com every single day. In doing so, he refined his writing, made more and more contacts and built a real and viable audience. He focused on creating articles for entrepreneurs that entertain and inspire. Day in and day out, Haden learned to "give first."

Today Jeff Haden is one of the most read writers for entrepreneurs on Inc.com and LinkedIn. He also has a best-selling book called The Motivation Myth. You can learn more about Jeff at JeffHaden.com.

CHAPTER 7

GIVE FIRST WITH PROMOTIONAL PREMIUMS

"For it is in giving that we receive."
St. Francis of Assisi

No book on "Success in the *Give First Economy*" would be complete without a chapter the "OG" of Give First Marketing… Promotional Products.

Created in back in the late 1800's, promotional products are often an overlooked part of the marketing toolbox. There are even some college professors that refuse to talk about Promo when it comes to marketing classes. This is short sighted, small-minded and frankly irresponsible.

Why? Because promotional products work…and it's not just my opinion. Study after study is proving it to be true. So much so, that I wrote an entire book (*Delivering Marketing Joy*) on the subject. I don't want to "re-litigate" the entire argument here. But I will include this one section from the book here.

I am sure every form of advertising is accused of "not working." As I heard once, "Just because you can't put the ball in the basket, doesn't mean there's a problem with basketball. Maybe you're just not good at it."

Promotional products do work. Many of us have known this for years. But more studies are coming out all the time that proves it. That's the best thing about marketers getting more interested in measuring ROI. We are getting facts to back up the theory. Here are just a few from a study released in 2010:

Of 1000 people surveyed who had received a promotional product, 89% could recall the advertiser. Say that out loud people. The name of the game in advertising is to create customer recall. Nearly 90% is a number that you might want to know when you are figuring your budget.

14.7% of participants reported contacting the advertiser after receiving the promotional product. That is nearly 3 times greater than other media.

When done right, promotional products are incredibly effective. The more the facts stack up, the harder it is to argue.

Work Too Well?

The great irony is the other side of the coin. Can it be argued that these products work too well? Don't believe me? Well look no further than the laws written to limit the amount of promotional materials that can be given in the healthcare industry to doctors. These laws were put in place because Big Pharmaceutical companies were creating "undue influence" over these physicians. Now some will argue that these laws were put in place because of free trips, game tickets, and extravagant dinners. Maybe so.

But then why legislate the kinds of products that can be given to doctors' offices? To put it simply, these laws were created because promotional products were having a huge influence on healthcare decisions.

The goal of any marketing campaign is to affect behavior change. When you can implement a campaign so effective that it needs to be legislated...you may want to consider that strategy to promote your organization!

Promotional products have been around since the late 1800's and I think sometimes this is part of the reason the results are discounted. Everyone wants to know the newest, hottest ways to reach customers. You should!

But don't sleep on the power of promotional products. Now more than ever, you need to include them in your marketing mix.

If promotional products work so well...how can you use them to help you grow in the *Give First Economy*? Let's dig into that.

Marketing They Say "Thank You" For

As we like to say in the promotional world, when you create a promotional campaign that works, your customers and prospects will thank you for your advertising! No disrespect to radio, or TV, or newspaper, or social media...but no one thanks you for advertising there!

So how do you create a promo campaign that works and resonates in the *Give First Economy*? Here are just four things to consider to make sure you hit the mark.

Don't Just Go Cheap

Probably the biggest mistake I see businesses of all shapes and sizes making is considering your promo ONLY on price. Of course, your budget has to be a part of the discussion! It should be. But just like in EVERY other area of your life, price should not be the only piece of information you consider.

If you are shopping for a car, most people do not just look at price. You consider the features you're interested in. You think about the reputation of the dealership. You consider whether you want to drive lots of miles (so gas mileage might factor in) or if you will be going off road or driving in the snow. If you only consider price, you will likely get a vehicle you are unhappy with. You want a vehicle that's a good value. It should meet your needs AND fit in your budget.

When you are considering a promotional piece, think about that item being a very real and tangible representative of your brand...because it is.

Consider Where It Will Be Used

Now that you have decided to create a promotional piece that is not just a cheap piece of junk (we all thank you), you should consider how and where the item will be used. Do you want your prospects or customers to have your branding around their office? Is that where these decisions are made? What about the kitchen? You would be surprised how many decisions are made there. Regardless, you need to consider your customer and where you can bring them value. When you spend just a little time to do that, you can come up with a promotional piece that is used, appreciated and valued for years to come!

Consider Advertising Versus Branding

Next, consider what you are trying to accomplish with the promotional piece. Sometimes, you want to provide your customers and prospects information where they can reach you. Maybe (and I am just spitballing here) you're a pizza place and you create a dry erase board for your best clients. You want them to place this on the fridge and have your phone number, website, etc. in front of them all the time. Great. This is more of an advertising or direct marketing approach.

But sometimes you just want to create more brand affinity...and there is a ton of power in that. You might want to create a super soft, comfy and cool t-shirt. This warm piece reminds your customers of their feelings for your brand every time they put it on. You aren't going to plaster your phone number all over the t-shirt (seriously, please don't). With a piece like this, you create more brand recognition. Done right, they will remember you.

By the way, neither of these is wrong. But it's important to understand what you are trying to accomplish when you begin.

Make It A Thank You Gift

One of my rules in sales is to (occasionally) go to your clients and prospects when you are NOT asking them for money! As entrepreneurs, salespeople and marketers, we are often guilty of following the rule of *Glengarry Glen Ross*. Remember that scene from the movie when Alec Baldwin declares "Coffee is for Closers!"

Baldwin stands at the chalkboard and yells at his underperforming sales team and shows them the ABC's of Selling.

A: Always

B: Be

C: Closing.

I disagree. (If you have made it this far in the book this should be no surprise).

Promotional products can be the perfect way to go to a client with a marketing gift just to say "thank you." Going to your client, on a regular basis, with a simple "thank you" and a small token of your appreciation for their support, will go a long way toward creating a long and profitable relationship.

Simply put, giving first is all about creating value for your customers and prospects. The best promotional campaigns are designed to do just that.

Now, let's meet Bill Petrie. But this time...Bill can tell the story himself!

GIVING FIRST WITH BILL PETRIE

After 15 years in the promotional marketing industry, I found myself at a career crossroads through no fault of my own. I had sold multi-million dollar programs to Fortune 500 clients, worked in executive leadership positions at some of the largest companies in the industry, and, most recently built a $6M promotional marketing division within a large office products company – a division that was recently closed due to corporate realignment. Despite my knowledge, experience, and success, I wasn't sure where I fit into the industry which, frankly, scared me to death.

After much self-reflection, I asked myself the same question many displaced professionals ask: "now what?"

To be clear, I had gone the traditional route of finding a job before and the prospect of doing that at 45 didn't excite me very much. After much internal debate and dialog, I decided to begin a consulting agency that would provide some moderate income as well as serve as an online resume of sorts. To truly set myself apart, I knew I couldn't call it "Bill Petrie Consulting" as that would simply underscore the fact that I was unemployed and, perhaps, unwanted. Instead, I merged the words branding and elevate to create, "brandivate." Even though brandivate was a front for finding a job, the name gave me a renewed a sense of purpose that simply being a consultant never would and I felt potential employers would take notice as well.

But how would I get brandivate noticed? If you've gone this far in the book, you already know the answer: I decided to give first.

Writing has always been a passion of mine, so I decided the best way to showcase my knowledge, expertise, and personality was to start a blog. Published every Monday and Thursday without fail, I wrote about sales, leadership, marketing, branding, and other business challenges while injecting my own personality. Sometimes the blogs were funny and irreverent while other times they were introspective and pointed. They were always, however, transparent and candid. It was freeing to share the thoughts that were in my head – and do so in a very public way. Over time, it helped rebuild my confidence because I was able to help so many people which, in turn, gave me the fuel needed to push even more.

Without sounding boastful, the thoughts I shared were very well received by the promotional marketing industry. What started off as a creative job seeking strategy turned into a viable company as many organizations hired me to help them with their challenges: marketing, sales, branding, and even logistics. Even more, I became a sought-after speaker both in and out of the industry, was elected to several industry boards, named the number one social media influence in the world of promotional products, and recognized as an industry thought leader. Eventually, I sold brandivate to PromoCorner where I now serve a President – and I still publish a weekly blog.

I attribute the success I achieved after launching brandivate because I made a commitment to consistently creating content and always giving first. By taking this approach, it made me realize that I received far more when I put other people's needs in front of my own. Giving first is a strategy that works as it not only makes you a better human but allows you to truly show you care about your target audience.

CHAPTER 8

GIVE KINDNESS

"Be Kind whenever possible. It's always possible."
The Dalai Lama

I grew up in a very small town in Ohio called Coshocton. It's the kind of town where everyone knows everyone. Coshocton had four small neighborhood elementary schools, back when people still walked to school. I am not sure of the exact grade, but it was in elementary school when I first heard of a girl we'll call Nancy.

Nancy was a young girl who, it turned out, was the same age as me. And as I learned from the other kids, Nancy was…not one of the pretty people. And unfortunately, that meant that kids made fun of her. As a matter of fact, for some time, while I was in elementary school, whenever anything was ugly, or smelly or disgusting, kids would say "That's Nancy."

This is the part of the story when people groan. I know, kids can be mean. It's the reason I roll my eyes when people act as if bullying is brand new. Unfortunately, that behavior has been going on forever.

This behavior continued for me until something changed.

All the four neighborhood schools combined to go the same Middle School. Middle School was 6th, 7th, and 8th grades, and all the kids you didn't know, now became your classmates. That's when I met Nancy.

I once heard, if you want to hate someone, don't get to the know them.

When I got to Middle School, I got to see Nancy, the person. Then and there, I made the decision to stop making fun of her. Now I want to be VERY clear. I did nothing else. I did not defend her. I didn't scold anyone for being mean. I didn't do anything, really. I just stopped being mean. That's it. That went on for several years, until Nancy and I graduated together in a class of just over 100 students.

I went off to college and didn't think about Nancy again for years.

Then, 4 years later I was back at home working at a local factory as a summer job. Like a lot of students, I spent the summer working to help make some money (and to remind me to study hard). I was at my second day and was at the breakroom when I was tapped on the shoulder. I turned around to see a short, stocky guy who looked like a brick layer. He looked strong and rough, and I was confused what he might want with me. Honestly, I thought he might have just wanted to mess with me.

"Are you Kirby Hasseman?", he asked in a gruff voice.

Thinking he was just going to haze me on my second day, I shot back, "Yeah."

Then he said, "I am Nancy's father."

I am sure my eyes got wide because my first reaction was "Oh shit. I am going to get my ass kicked on the second day of work!"

Then his face softened, and he said something I will never forget. "I just wanted to say thank you."

Now I was really confused.

He continued, "The kids in school were always mean to Nancy. But she said you were always kind to her. I appreciate that. So, thank you." And with that, he walked away.

I was stunned. And to this day, that absolutely breaks my heart. I was NEVER kind to Nancy. I was, at best, polite. I was not kind. I was just less awful.

There she was, struggling to get through school, while people insulted her. And she thought I was kind. Just think of what I could have done if I had ACTUALLY been kind.

Kindness Is A Gift

We are at a time in our culture when we have a deficiency of kindness. People are more depressed and anxious and frustrated than at any time in our history. In a time, when we are more technologically connected than ever before, we feel lonelier.

Why is that? I think it's because we lack real and genuine connection.

How can we bridge that gap? Real, honest, kindness.

And here's the thing...based on the story above...we know the bar is just not very high. We have come to a place where a lack of malice is perceived as kindness. So, to be honest, if you are not able to manage that, why the hell not?

When you take the time to give a smile, a kind word, a hug or just some time, you can create real connections by making people feel special...because they are.

What Does Kindness Look Like?

The concept of Kindness can be a little bit nebulous. What does it mean? What does it look like? Because of that, it's easy to either be intimidated by it or forget about it. But we all know kindness when we see it. And though it can be the "Random Act of Kindness" when you buy a stranger's food in the drive-thru, there are many other ways to spread kindness as well. And here's the thing about "random" acts of kindness, if you are not intentional about it, random can become "never". Here are a few simple ways to give kindness every day.

Give A Smile: When is the last time you dropped a child off at school? Have you ever looked at the faces of the other parents? There are so many faces of stressed, frustrated, unhappy people. I make it a point to smile at those that look at me. Often, it surprises people. When they notice, it often causes a smile in return.

This can be powerfully true in business. So many of us are lost in our own heads, grinding and chasing our goals that we have a constant look of consternation. It's our business RBF (Resting Bitch Face). Taking a moment to give everyone you encounter a smile is an act of kindness.

Give Some Time: By the same token, most of us are always on the go. We are a culture that is constantly "busy." So much so, that the word busy has become a badge of honor. The point, my friends, is not to be busy. It's to be productive (but that could be another rant altogether). One way to be more productive is to create real and lasting connections with your customers and your prospects...and that takes time.

Giving your time is an act of kindness. It shows the other person that they are more important than your phone or your next appointment. Whether it's with your child, a non-profit you are passionate about, or a friend, give them time.

Really Listen: As an add on to the last point, a real act of kindness is truly listening. Spending time with someone is incredible, but if you are the one doing all the talking, you might be missing the point. I know, because I struggle with this all the time! I often need to remind myself to shut my mouth and dig into what they are saying. Really listening is a kindness. And as my wife will tell you, if I stop talking, that is a kindness too!

So hopefully you can see that giving kindness is not hard. It's not expensive. It's a mindset. Kindness is a secret weapon too, because just like giving out **Joy** in previous chapters, you can stand out. Most people are simply not practicing kindness in a consistent way.

Does Kindness Really Matter?

Now maybe you are thinking, "This is great. It all sounds nice. But can it really make a difference?" In a word, yes.

I am reminded of a story I heard the author, Wayne Dyer, tell years ago. I will do my best to recap the concept here. It starts with a study on Random Acts of Kindness.

Let's start with what they were measuring...oxytocin. Oxytocin is a hormone that exists in most species. In humans it's known as the bonding hormone. When released it can reduce stress, fear and anxiety. It also increases trust and is often called "the love hormone". It has a host of other positive effects on the body.

Scientists wanted to study Random Acts of Kindness, and how they affected the level of oxytocin in the body. Here's what they found.

When someone received a Random Act of Kindness, a predictably good thing happened. They received a boost in oxytocin. Makes sense, right? They felt good. That's great...and that's why we do the act of kindness. We want to make the other person feel good. Mission accomplished.

What the researchers also found, however, is the person who GAVE the random act of kindness got an equal boost of the oxytocin! So, by doing something for someone else, it makes YOU feel good. This makes sense too, I think. When we do something nice for someone else, though it might not have been the goal, it does make us feel better. That is great.

But here's the best part.

Researchers found that people who "observed" the Random Act of Kindness were affected, too. This person did not receive the gift or give it. They just happened to be there. They watched it happen. Those people received an equal boost of oxytocin as well! To me, this is incredible. If you just watch someone being kind, it makes you feel better.

So, when people say that we can't make a difference by a simple act of kindness, science tells us they are wrong.

SIMPLE (NOT EASY) GIVE FIRST TACTICS

"Life is simple, not easy."
Author unknown.

If you have made it this far, you've undoubtedly had a moment when you said, "Well, sure. I know that!"

You do. But as I said before, "The greatest distance in the world is the distance between, "I know" and "I do." So often in life, we know what we need to do. We just fail to consistently act upon it.

Most of the time, the answer to the question is right in front of us. The way to improve is simple. It's the reason that it's often easy to solve other people's challenges! It's simple. When you look at someone else's challenge from the outside, without emotion, it's easy to diagnose the problem and the solution. It's so simple!

"Just get up earlier!"

"You just need to leave him/her."

"Quit your job."

"Start writing!"

"Make more sales calls."

But inevitably, though we know what the solution is (or someone has pointed it out to us) it's hard to execute. We know what to do. We might even "want" to do the right thing. But when the alarm clock goes off, or the moment of truth comes, we fall back into our old habits.

So, as we look at some specific tactics to create Success in the *Give First Economy*, let's remember this. These tactics can seem basic. You probably already know you should be doing them. But most of us are not doing them...at least not consistently. If that's the case with you, let's use this chapter as the reminder on the wall to "get back to basics".

Send ACTUAL Thank You Cards

When talking about this topic in front of audiences, I always ask a simple question - "Where do you open your mail?" After some puzzled looks, many participants say, "Over the trash can."

They do this, and you might too, because our mailbox has become overrun with mail that we do NOT want. We get bills, marketing flyers, sales offers, advertisements and, of course, credit card offers. What we don't get any more is personal mail. We don't get letters and we don't get thoughtful, sincere thank you notes. We don't get these because it's much easier to send an email or a text. That's cool. I use those all the time. But they are not personal, and they are not special. Your customers rarely are surprised or delighted to see another email from you. They're just trying to delete the emails as fast as they come in. You don't stand out in the inbox. As a matter of fact, you are probably just another annoyance.

A thank you card is different. And remember, in the minds of our customer, better is not better. Different is better.

In the *Give First Economy*, a thank you card is slow, and expensive, and inconvenient (to send) ...and that makes it special.

P.S. I need to continue to get better at this too!

Go to People When You Are NOT Asking For Money

As salespeople, entrepreneurs, and marketers, we are always going to people to show them what we have to sell. That makes sense! We are excited about our product or offering, so we should be. As a matter of fact, if you really believe your product will help your customers and prospects, I think you have a moral obligation to show them.

But there is a caveat.

If you want your customers and prospects to really trust you, you need to show them they are more than a number. They can't just be a number or a means to an end. The best salespeople develop real and lasting relationships that last past the transaction. It's hard to do that when you are always "selling."

What does that look like? Simple (but not easy) ...go to them when you are not selling anything.

Stop in occasionally just to say "thank you" for the support.

Share an article that is related to their industry or interest. (One of my clients is a huge New York Giants fan, so I share cool stories with him about that team).

Invite them to lunch just to catch up.

These activities are not necessarily efficient, or measurable…but they are powerful.

One thing to note though. If you are making a point to have a "non-sales" contact…don't sell. Don't take the time on the way out to mention "oh, one thing on sales is…". That ruins it. The idea of this contact is you are not selling. You are building the personal relationship.

The sales pitch at the end changes everything. I struggle with this one. I am always in a state of selling. But when you add that last thing, you take away the friend vibe you have built. The business will often come to you anyway. The client might bring it up. But if you want to make it a non-sales call…don't sell.

Recommend Things You Don't Sell

This was a game changer for me. For many years, I was a salesperson in the Promotional Products industry. That is what I sold. Maybe you have heard the saying, "When you have a hammer, everything looks like a nail." This was certainly true for me. No matter what the campaign, issue or event, a promotional product was the hammer I was swinging to drive it home.

Then one day I was working with a friend. This was a person who was looking at me as a real advisor. They had a campaign coming up and had asked for my advice on the best way to go to market. I made my normal recommendations (promotional products), then I asked, "Have you thought about radio?". I talked to him about creating a short-term blitz campaign to help raise awareness.

He was surprised. "Do you sell radio?"

> **"No," I said. "I just think that might be a way to boost this for you." He appreciated it. I was making a recommendation based on his success not mine.**

You can, and should, do the same thing in your business. It's your job (and as I said, obligation) to help your prospects and customers with your offerings. But when you take a step back and recommend what is best for them, regardless of whether you do it or not, you provide so much more value.

And when you do it, you move from being a salesperson to being an advisor.

Create Content

I spent an entire chapter on this, so I won't take too much time. But when you create content that REALLY provides value to your audience, you are giving first. That is why the best content has the audience in mind.

Content is not an advertisement. Content is not a sales offer. It's important that you do those things, but don't mistake them as the same thing.

Refer back to the 4 C's of Content and start to create content that positions you as the expert.

Curate Content

If you have been reading the message on creating content with an internal groan, I might be able to let you off the hook (a little bit). Though I still believe that the best way to position yourself as an expert in your respected field is to create the content, there is another simple way to add value through content.

Curate the best and share with your audience.

There is more and more content being created today than ever. In every field of expertise, there are voices that are working to add value just as I have suggested. They are writing blogs, producing videos and recording podcasts. Once you have engaged with them (with the "power of the wink"), become the person that shares them to your audience.

The best curators often add their own comment or review of the content and directs their audience to check it out. The original writer will love it (as long as you give them complete credit) because they are increasing their audience. And if you do this consistently, you will become the "go to" place to go for this topic for your customers and prospects.

In addition, you can also curate special content just for your best customers. For example, your expertise might be in marketing. But if you have clients that are in the tech space, it might make sense to think of them when you read a particularly interesting article about their field. Send it to them with a thoughtful note. You might even ask them what they think about it to continue to broaden the relationship.

It will make them feel more important and you might learn something too!

Create Targeted Branded Merchandise

I wrote an entire chapter on this, so you know I think it's important. But if you truly want to take advantage of the *Give First Economy*, it's worth mentioning one more time. You want to create thoughtful and targeted branded merchandise to your best customers and prospects. It is the very definition of "give first" marketing.

But don't just fall into the trap of giving away "CPS." That cheap plastic shit is what gives the promo industry a bad name, and it will do the same for brand. Just like nearly every other thing, when it comes to branded merchandise, you get what you pay for. This does not mean you need to overspend. It means you need to be intentional. Create branded merchandise that actually represents your brand and brings value to your customers.

If you do that, you are sure to stand out in a crowded marketplace with marketing that your clients actually appreciate!

When I read a book or attend a seminar, I want some actual tactics that I can put into play immediately to help me grow my business, or myself. This list was created with the goal to get you started right away.

Good luck. And let me know what other tactics you have that can help you create success in the *Give First Economy*!

PART 2
GET MORE STUFF DONE

If you have gotten this far in the book, congratulations! You are well on your way to standing out in a crowded marketplace. There are more and more voices creating more and more noise in the market today. By now, hopefully you recognize that by "giving first" you can start to stand out…in a good way.

But as I have talked to audiences all over the country about this topic, the one push back I most often get is, "I love the concept, but this sounds like it's going to take a lot of extra time!"

At first, I was surprised by this objection.

I mean, of course it's going to take extra time! Nearly every <u>real</u> tactic and strategy you can do that will actually affect your business will take time. It will be hard. It will take work. The idea that there is some "easy button" people can push to take their business and their lives to the next level is a fallacy. It doesn't exist.

Let me save you some time. Stop looking for the easy way. There is no easy way. It takes work.

That is the reason for Part 2 of this book.

After being asked (over and over and over) how I am able to implement these strategies, I worked to answer the question, "How do you get so much stuff done"? When I hear that question, I know I'm on the right track.

What I love about Part 2 is, though these concepts are based on my experience, they are not based on my opinion. These are science-based strategies designed to help you get more accomplished each and every day. Some of them are a bit counter-intuitive, but I will explain the science and the practice...and how they have affected me as well.

These are going to be fast paced and quick. I will talk about things you need to start doing right away in order to increase your productivity. And I will give you some things you need to stop doing right away as well. The goal is to help you "get more stuff done" so you can "give out more good.'"

Let's dig into Part 2 of the book: How to Get More stuff Done.

CHAPTER 10

START TO GET MORE SLEEP

"If you end your day feeling like you got nothing done, it's because you weren't working; you were busy, not productive."
Richie Norton

Let's start this section on getting more done by getting rid of a huge myth. The art of being more productive is not about (just) getting more stuff done. It's about getting the right things done. We don't need to just jam more and more random activity into your calendar.

That's the art of being busy…and it's dangerous.

We have an entire culture of people who believe that being busy is the goal. It's not. The idea is to do the difficult and productive work of chasing our dreams and goals. And the reality is, busy people don't do that. Productive people do.

So, let's talk about what you need to do to get more work that matters done. You need your brain.

Sure, there are jobs in the world where you don't need to use your brain. But the number of those jobs are declining. And more importantly, the value of those jobs is declining. Robots can do them. The kind of work that is creative and powerful and makes a difference in the world, requires brain work.

To do your best work, you need your brain to be working at the top of its game.

It's the great fallacy of college, isn't it? Every semester, when I was in college, finals week would roll around, and a campus full of smart people would become zombies. They would cram and pull "all-nighters" trying to cram as much information into their brains as they could so they could get a high grade on their final exam.

It turns out that this is exactly the opposite way to make your brain work well. If you want your brain to perform at an optimum level, you (and your brain) need proper rest.

Start Getting More Sleep

According to the book *Brain Rules*, by John Medina, one of the most powerful things you can do to make your brain work smarter is to get sleep. Though each of us needs a different amount of sleep to operate optimally, most Americans are not getting enough. We stay up late and get up early with the idea that we can get more done. In reality, it's making us dumb.

According to Medina, if you are person that needs 8 hours sleep (and most of us do), getting substantially less can decrease brain function by up to 40%. That is a big number! In addition, if you follow up that first night with a second night of sleep deprivation, you decrease your brain function by up another 40%! I tell people, if I go for a third night, I am nothing but a talking monkey.

What does this mean for you?

With decreased sleep, your brain works slower. You are less creative. You're less able to deal with stress and more likely to become angry. There are even studies that show that a person dealing with prolonged sleep deprivation is similar to one that is drunk. It's not my opinion folks. It's how the brain and body work.

We all want to get more done. But it's about operating at an optimal level so you can get the best work done. If you want to create your best work, you need to get enough rest. If you want to deal with stress and think creatively, your brain needs sleep.

If you are like most of us in the world today, you need to be thinking faster. Getting the proper rest can help you move faster and smarter while you're awake.

CHAPTER 11

START TO GET MORE EXERCISE

"The mind is just like a muscle - the more you exercise it, the stronger it gets and the more it can expand."
Idowu Koyenikan

Now that you have properly rested your brain and your body, it is time to put it through the paces! If you want to be more productive and happier, it's time to start a regular exercise routine.

Wait! Don't stop reading yet! Even if you are not someone who likes to spend hours in the gym, this still means you.

Getting more exercise does not mean you need to pump tons of iron or run 5 marathons a year! It means, if you want to function at your highest level, you need to get moving and get your blood pumping for 20-30 minutes each day. (I like to get started first thing in the morning).

There are countless books and articles about the benefits of exercise for the body. We already know this is true. This falls under that category of "The greatest distance in the world is the distance between 'I know' and 'I do'." We know we should be exercising to be more physically fit. And even those of us that exercise regularly, would probably admit to needing to exercise more.

This is not about getting 6 pack abs. It's about making your brain function at its highest level. Most of us have had that time, during or after a long walk or a workout, when we came up with a really cool idea. You might have been focusing on the problem at hand, or even had your mind wandering, and then—boom—you have a cool idea. This happens for a reason.

I am going to lean on the book, *Brain Rules* again.

Whether you know it or not, blood is constantly being pumped to your brain. It's being delivered by blood vessels. These blood vessels are like the highways into your brain, delivering blood. The better the blood flow to your brain, the better your brain works.

When you exercise, it makes sense that the blood is pumping faster.

But more importantly, as you exercise the blood vessels are being improved. It's like the highways to the brain are being paved. That way the blood is being delivered more efficiently and at a higher rate.

But wait, there's more…and this is the best part.

In addition to the highways being paved, the act of exercise actually creates new highways! That's right, new roads are being created into your brain to deliver more blood.

So, in essence, the act of exercising actually makes you smarter! Is that incredible or what?

As we discussed in the previous chapter, if we want to be more productive (and get more done), we need our brain to function at the highest rate it can. Exercise can help your brain function more effectively and creatively.

When you combine this with the fact that exercise will give you the ability to have more energy and deal with stress better, it becomes something that goes from "Yeah, I should do that more often" to "I have to do that each day."

We will talk more in a bit about how to build this into your daily routine. But for now, just know that you need to start working in working out.

Exercise will make you smarter.

CHAPTER 12

START BEING INTENTIONAL

*"If you don't know where you are going,
any road will take you there."*

Stop me if you heard this one before: "I want to do it, but I just don't have time". Or what about this one, "Where does the day go?" Or have you ever thought (or said), "Wow I was busy all day, but what did I actually get done?"

If you say you haven't heard (or thought) any of these, you are a liar. We have all said them...at least to ourselves. It's the symptom of letting your day--or your life--happen to you. You might have been hustling. You were certainly busy. But you were not intentional.

You did not live "on purpose."

Don't worry; this is a judgment-free zone. We have all done it. I have most certainly had those days where I came home exhausted and frazzled and ready for a drink...but was not sure where the day went.

That is why we need to spend some time to create our day (and ultimately our business) intentionally (on purpose). Be we can do better than that. In order to take this intentionality to the next level, we can also create a business mission too (on purpose). When you combine the two, great things can really happen.

Let's start with Intentionality.

It is amazing how many well-meaning, intelligent and somewhat successful people go through their daily lives and routines while life "just happens to them". They work hard. They do their best at their jobs. But at the end of the day, their hustle is misguided—or more accurately—unguided.

Studies show that only 3 percent of people have goals. Even less of them actually write them down! That is beyond mind blowing to me. If you don't know where you are going, how can you get there? What are the next steps? How could I (or anyone else) help you? By simply spending some "me time" to consider your goals, you are ahead of most of the population.

Side note, I think sometimes people don't participate in goal setting because you might feel foolish or wrong. But keep in mind; you can change your goals. You can update them. But you can't create a road map if you don't know where you are going.

Now let's talk for a moment about goals.

As we talk about being intentional, we really mean setting real goals. So, if you are a person that has not taken the time to set (or write down) goals in the past...where do you start? I recommend starting with the 5 F's.

The 5 F's

When most of us do start talking about goals we tend to focus on two areas in our life. We focus on finance and fitness? Am I right? We either want to make more money, pay off our bills, or drop 20 pounds and have 6-pack abs. There is nothing wrong with those goals, but the focus is pretty narrow in our lives.

> **If you want to have a well-rounded life, you should have well-rounded goals. You want to be intentional in other areas of your life too. That's why I came up with the 5 F's of goals in my life. The 5 F's help me look at the important areas of my life and set goals there.**

The 5 F's are:

Finance

Fitness

Family

Faith

Fun

When I'm coming up with my personal goals, I like to have at least one goal that excites me in each of these areas. When I have those, then I know I am working to be intentional in every area of my life that matters to me.

So, what does this actually look like? Here are some ideas in each area that can get you started.

Finance: This is the area of your life where you can look at increasing your income, creating more savings, starting retirement, increasing sales, paying off debt and creating financial freedom. Break these down. What do these look like to you?

Fitness: This might be a goal to drop a certain number of pounds, or it might be a challenge to finish a 10k race. You might look at doing 100 push-ups a day or keeping your caloric intake down.

Family: Do you want to have a family dinner night each week? Do you want to take a vacation with your squad? For me, I remind myself to be a better father and husband.

Faith: For some people, this might start by creating a prayer or meditation practice. For others it might mean you become a leader in your church.

Fun: Yes…I think we should all have goals that bring us joy. It's the point of the exercise. Create some goals on your list that just make you smile!

Why I Don't Love SMART Goals

Whenever you start to look at any exercise on goal setting (and being intentional) the idea of SMART goals comes up. And although I like the idea of giving people a framework around goal setting, so they can get started, I don't love SMART goals. Not sure what I am talking about? Here is the basic definition of a SMART goal.

To make your goal **S.M.A.R.T.,** *it needs to conform to the following criteria: Specific, Measurable, Attainable, Relevant and Timely.*

As I said, I understand the basic framework. In addition, I think it makes sense to compare your goals to this list in order to audit yourself. Are you saying you want to "get fit"? Then looking at this list might remind you to be more specific. What does "get fit" mean? In that way, this can be really helpful.

On the other hand, though I understand the idea of a goal being measurable, I don't ALWAYS think it has to be. For example, my number one goal each year is to be a better father and husband. I don't know how I should measure that. But when I have that goal written down, at the top of my list, and sitting on my desk each day, it helps to remind me the kind of man I want to be.

I mention this because I think goals are extremely personal.

What might excite me, might bore the hell out of Mark Cuban (or you). Your goals are yours alone. You need to be self-aware enough to create them just for you.

Final Note on Goals: Self Awareness

That leads nicely into the way you create goals for you. I am a believer in big, audacious goals. I like to stretch myself. Then, if I don't reach these lofty goals, I feel like I went farther than I would have gone had I not aimed high. I want to think big because it excites me. And I know I will not get completely discouraged by falling a bit short.

One of my sales team members does NOT feel this way. He knows that if he sets goals that are too high, and he falls short, he will become discouraged quickly. It will become a negative and he might give up. He likes to set smaller, incremental goals, that he can achieve and surpass.

In my opinion, neither of us are wrong.

As I said, goals are personal. There is no wrong way to set goals. They are for you...not anyone else. I think this is one of the reasons people shy away from writing goals down. They think they are "doing it wrong." You are not.

The only way you fail in goal setting is if you fail to set goals.

If you want to be more productive. If you want your life to be more purposeful and (dare I say) happy, you need to START being intentional.

Stop reading now. Take some time. Go and write down your goals... then start chasing them. Good luck!

CHAPTER 13

START A MORNING ROUTINE

"The moment you take responsibility for everything in your life is the moment you can change anything in your life." Hal Elrod

Let me paint you a picture. Every morning at about the same time, I wander into our local hospital. It's a small-town hospital, and it is usually fairly quiet. I nod hello to a few people as I walk through the two sliding doors and then take a quick left… into the cafeteria.

I stride quickly into the food preparation area and say hello to the person behind the counter. Regardless of which person who is making the food, they set straight to making my breakfast. They don't have to ask what I am having. I get the same thing every day.

Once I see they have started my eggs, I head over to the counter to pay for my breakfast. They ring it up (again, without asking) and I pay for my breakfast. Then I head back over to the food prep area to wait.

I do this every day.

Now some might see this as monotonous, (and some people have told me) but this is a routine I have created very much on purpose. It's one piece of my morning routine that helps to get my day started on the right foot. I don't want to leave it to chance.

Here's the thing. Science will tell you that your brain is functioning at its highest abilities for around the first 3 hours you are awake. Once you have wiped the sleep from your eyes, your brain is rested and on high alert.

Now ask yourself this, "What am I using this prime brain time for?"

Many of us fill our mornings with mundane, non-essential tasks. We get the kids ready for school. We check Facebook. We read emails. We watch TV. We do just about anything except work to chase the things that are most important to us!

It's no wonder you are not achieving more of your goals. The best part of your day is wasted on other people's agendas!

That is why it is SO important to create Intentional Morning Routines.

When I am speaking to groups, I always ask "How many of you love to wake up in the morning and throw your running shoes on and hit the treadmill?" Inevitably there are a few weary hands that go up. With a great deal of disdain in my voice I say "Well, good for you!"

I am not one of these people. I have tried, repeatedly, to start a workout routine that begins with me rolling out of bed in the dark, putting on my running shoes and hitting the gym. Each and every time, I continue for about a week, then I stop. I hate it.

On the other hand, I know it's important for me to have some exercise as a part of my morning routine. So, I have worked to create a morning routine that works for me. It helps me to do the important things I know I should do…in a way that I will actually do them. It's all about a routine that works for me.

Oh, and by getting these important things done in the morning, we don't rely as much on willpower to get things done at the end of the day. This matters a ton. Why? Because willpower is a finite resource.

We beat ourselves up all the time because we are weak when we can't keep up on a diet, or writing a book, or starting a business. We know we have time at the end of the day to "write the next chapter" or "get on the treadmill". But after a long day, we struggle to maintain the motivation. All we want to do is come home, put our feet up, and have a cookie or a beer. I totally get it. You are not weak…and you are not alone.

You are just working with a finite resource. Your willpower gets weaker as the day goes on. The more decisions you have to make, the less you want to make them later in the day. The more you expend mental and physical energy during the day, the less you want to do it at night. That's why you tend to make those "bad" decisions at the end of the day. You're tired.

That's why it's so important to stack the deck in your favor! By positioning the things you know you want (and need) to do first thing in the day, you get the chance to take late day willpower out of the equation. Not only do you get to use your best brain on the task, you get to start your day with a sense of accomplishment too!

Here is what my morning routine looks like:

Get Up! As soon as the alarm goes off, I get out of bed. My alarm is just out of reach, so I have to stand up to turn it off. I also get up before my wife. This is great for me because I don't want the alarm to disturb her. It's good motivation to make the beeping stop!

Make Coffee and Let the Dogs Out: This is when I am most groggy. So, I make the same amount of coffee each morning. While it is brewing, I take the time to take my pups outside. This is another simple step to help me wake up.

Read and Write: As I drink my coffee and continue to wake up, I like to fill my brain with some good stuff. Often, I head to blogs that inspire me to get my brain working. It's also the time when I work on writing for my own blog or books. Pushing out good into the world helps to inspire me too.

Exercise: At this point, I have probably been up an hour. I have read and had my coffee. Now I head to exercise. This is the point that I have found (for me) that I *want* to exercise. It's not so much of a chore. That means I don't have to fight it. I look forward to it! And although this helps me stay more fit, my goal here is to continue to prime my brain.

Shower and Meditation: Now I take the time to cool off and get in the shower. I know meditation is important (more on that in a second) and this is where I can consistently find time for that in my morning.

Breakfast: And we are back to the beginning! Each morning I get my protein with scrambled eggs and bacon…and then I am ready to head into the office to attack the day.

This is my morning routine. It's not prescriptive. You need to set up your morning so that it works best for you. What I do know is that if you get the most important things scheduled in the first part of your day, the rest of your day will be more productive too!

CHAPTER 14

START GIVING YOURSELF HEADSPACE

"The quieter you become, the more you hear."

Let's start with a confession. I struggle with this. I have a high motor, and for years, the idea of sitting quietly with my legs crossed keeping my mind devoid of any thoughts not only sounded impossible, it sounded like one of the 7 circles of hell.

There is no way I could do it…right?

The problem was, it seemed like every time I read something about someone I admired, the word meditation came up. They talked about how it helped them be more creative, or relieve stress, or sleep better. It forced me to look in the mirror. Could I meditate?

In a word, yes.

Let's start by blowing up one important myth of meditation. You don't need to clear your mind of thoughts. That is not the point at all. And it's probably the biggest reason most people give up in the first place. They think they are "doing it wrong." The book, *Meditation for Fidgety Skeptics*, helped me with this so much.

We can't stop or control our thoughts, but we *can* decide how much attention to give them. It's about taking the time to separate your thoughts from you. I love what the Chopra Center says about this:

When Chopra Center co-founder, Dr. David Simon taught meditation, he would often tell students, "The thought *I'm having thoughts* may be the most important thought you have ever thought, because before you had that thought, you **may** not have even known you were having thoughts. You probably thought you *were* your thoughts." Simply noticing that you are having thoughts is a breakthrough because it begins to shift your internal reference point from ego mind to witnessing awareness.

We live in a world that is more and more overloaded with stimulus that seems to be fighting for our attention. Between 24-hour news (which is mostly negative remember), endless entertainment options, social media and our phones, so many of us never take the time to disconnect. We never take the time to "just be."

This is where a practice of meditation (and prayer) can help.

"Great," you might be thinking. "What does this have to do with "getting more done?" As it turns out, a lot. And as we have talked about already…it all comes back to your brain.

More and more studies are showing that a regular meditation practice can help to decrease stress, decrease anxiety, improve sleep, help with creative thinking and so much more.

The push back I get (and have given in the past) is simple. I don't have time. Sure, I love the idea of decreasing my stress, but who has time to sit around for hours and "just be?"

That's another myth. It doesn't have to take forever. In the book I mentioned earlier, *Meditation for Fidgety Skeptics*, author Dan Harris argues that even 1 minute of meditation can help. Most experts argue that there are enhanced benefits when meditating longer, but don't use that as an excuse not to do it at all.

Even the busiest person (yes, even you) has a minute to spare.

One good way to begin meditating is with some help. I started with the app, Headspace. It gave me 10 guided meditations to get me started. Each of the sessions were 10 minutes long. It was an amazing introduction into what meditation was…and what it was not.

As I said when I started the chapter, I still struggle with this. That's why morning routines are so important for me. I have created a short window in the shower in the morning when I can give meditation my attention. By doing so, I don't have to create that space someplace else in my day.

Want to be happier and more productive? It might be time to give yourself some headspace.

CHAPTER 15

START A PRACTICE OF GRATITUDE

"The simplest and most powerful way to neutralize our negative thinking is through the daily practice of gratitude."

There is one formula we have all wrong in our culture. We think that if we work hard and we gain success, we will be happy. So many of us have bought into this failed formula and it looks like this:

Hard Work + Success = Happiness

It's just wrong. You and I both know it. The problem is this formula can deliver happiness for a moment. There is a short window of happiness (maybe) when you reach your goal. But then it becomes the new normal, and that boost of dopamine goes away.

Then you are left with a bit of an empty feeling. Was that it? Or worse yet, you never really get that boost at all. As I said, it's a failed formula.

We need to rethink the equation like this:

Happiness + Hard Work = Success

In his wonderful book *The Happiness Equation*, Neil Pasricha gives study after study that shows that the human brain simply performs better when it is happy. Students performed better on tests, people were more successful in their jobs, and in my favorite study, doctors were more accurate! In one example, when doctors were given a lollipop before going into to see a patient (they were not allowed to eat it as the sugar might affect the results) their diagnosis were more accurate!

Take that in for just a moment.

Doctors, some of the most educated people on the planet, were better at their job if they were given a small boost of positivity before they were asked to meet with a patient! If it's true for them, it is probably true for you. You are more likely to succeed if you give yourself a "boost of happiness" before you set out to take on a task.

But what if you are not in a good mood? Or better yet, what happens if you are not a naturally "rainbows and sunshine" happy person? Are you just screwed?

As you might expect, no you are not.

There are many ways to improve your mood before you take on a task. You can think about a place that brings you joy. Yes, the movie *Happy Gilmore* had something of value in it! You can go to your "happy place." You can picture yourself succeeding at the task. You can give yourself a lollipop and put it in your pocket.

You can do a lot of things to "boost your happy." But there is one thing that works better than anything else.

Start Being Grateful.

The quickest way I know to get my mind right and to restore my perspective is to go through a gratitude exercise. The fact is, nearly all of us have an immense of amount of good in our lives to be grateful for. We woke up today. We have some place to live. We have people in our life. Whatever. Spend the time and start listing the good things in your life (past and present) and it can help recalibrate your mind.

As a matter of fact, I try to do this right as I wake up in the morning... especially when I am stressed. It helps me start the day off on the right foot. The gratitude helps to decrease my stress. It helps to reframe me so I can live "in the now."

When you are being truly grateful, you can't be negative. Here's another formula for you:

Grateful = Happy

Want to keep the grateful train going? Here is another exercise to try. It's the 60-Day Gratitude Challenge. It's simple. For 30 days in a row, get up in the morning and write someone a thank you note. Every day. Tell them how much you appreciate them. Explain why they inspire you. Let them know how they helped you.

Here's the thing. At first, this will be fairly easy for many of us. There will be some "low hanging fruit" in our lives. These are the people who have helped us and continue to help us all of the time. But then, you will reach the end of this "easy" list...and you will have to start looking.

Then a magical thing will happen.

As you spend every day looking for something to be grateful for, you will start to see them! This can be eye opening for people. They start the exercise thinking there is no way they have this much in their life to be thankful for. Then, good things start to show up everywhere.

I call it the Red Toyota effect.

Have you ever noticed that after you buy a new car, you start to see cars just like it everywhere? You had never seen a Red Toyota like it... and now they seem to be around every corner! The reason is simple, you have told your subconscious mind that it was important. Now it is taking every opportunity to show it to you.

The same thing will happen with good things in your life. Most of us have an embarrassment of riches in our life. Most of us are truly blessed. But in the hustle and bustle of life, we just don't take the time to slow down and appreciate it.

We "know" the things are there. Intellectually, we understand that we are blessed in many ways. But we don't take the time to internalize it. We don't take the time to be truly grateful for it. This exercise makes you look. It makes you point it out. And, with the writing of each card, it makes you express that gratitude as well.

So, if gratitude makes you happy and happy makes you more likely to succeed...what are you waiting for? It's time to START a Daily Practice of Gratitude.

CHAPTER 16

START TAKING ACTION

"Hesitation is the kiss of death. You might hesitate for just a nanosecond, but that's all it takes. That one small hesitation triggers a mental system that's designed to stop you. And it happens in less than —you guessed it—five seconds."
Mel Robbins

Let me start this chapter by telling you something you already know. Nothing happens until someone takes action. No sales happen until someone makes the call. Nobody loses any weight until they start to work out. No one grows personally without putting in some work.

It all takes work. And, especially at the very beginning, it takes the courage to simply take action.

It's the reason that I talk about that quote so much.

The greatest distance in the world is the distance between "I know" and "I do." Most of us know what we need to do to get ahead. The majority of people know the life they want to lead. Most of us know what we want to say.

We just don't take action. We don't "do."

(And on a personal note, it's why it's taken me so damn long to write this chapter. I know what to do. I just have not done it. None of us are immune to this).

That's why this may be the most powerful START chapter of all. If you take all the lessons in this book in, and you don't put anything into action, then this was all just a fun intellectual exercise. Nothing will change unless you change it.

In the amazing book, *The 5 Second Rule*, Mel Robbins explains why this is true. When we set a goal, we tell our brain that it is important. (You did take the time to do that, right?) We have armed our subconscious brain and told it to help us reach that goal. That is why, when you set a goal to get more fit, you get an urge to work out when you walk by the gym. It might be subtle, but you get that nudge that you should go in there. You "know" it's the right thing to do if you want to reach that goal.

But then something happens. You hesitate. And as you do, your brain starts to come up with every reason why you should NOT go into the gym. And, according to Robbins, you have 5 seconds to take action, or your brain will completely talk you out of it!

If you are like me, you know this is true. Hundreds (if not thousands) of times throughout my life, this has happened to me. I know I should go workout in the morning, but I talk myself out of it. Or more often, I know I need to make that sales call. They are a prospect that I would really love to do business with, but as soon as I think about it, my brain starts to come up with excuses of why this is a terrible idea. These excuses come out of the woodwork like...

*You need another cup of coffee to get your energy up.

*Your script is not tight enough.

*They don't want to talk to you this early in the day.

*They don't want to talk to you this late in the day.

*They probably already have someone that...

You get the idea. These excuses roll around in my head until I decide that I will get to that call later...and I move on. Unfortunately, most of the time, the excuses come back the next time too.

Real Estate investor, author and speaker, Grant Cardone, compares this fear (and make no mistake, it is fear) to fire.

Cardone says that fire is fueled by oxygen. If you get a small fire going and you give it oxygen, it grows stronger and stronger until it gets out of control. But if you take away any oxygen, the fire dies out quickly.

Fear, on the other hand, is fueled with time. So, when you feel that urge to take action toward your goal, you will feel the fear. It makes sense, you are likely about to step outside of your comfort zone. But as you let your brain play through those excuses above, you give that fear time. The fear grows until you absolutely KNOW that this is not the right time to make that sales call. It will be a disaster.

So, you move on...and never take the action needed to move you.

I think what is important is to start looking at that fear as a sign that you are on the right track. When you feel it, you know you are pushing in the right direction. You get that feeling. You know you are about to go outside of your comfort zone. That is NOT a sign you need to stop. It's a sign you need to lean in.

As Mel Robbins would tell you, count backwards 5-4-3-2-1...and take action.

Regardless of the goals you have set for your life, no matter the obstacles that are in your way, nearly everything you want to move toward in your life will be aided by you taking the action to move forward.

CHAPTER 17

STOP HITTING THE SNOOZE BUTTON

"If you think about it, hitting the snooze button in the morning doesn't even make sense. It's like saying "I hate getting up in the morning —so I do it over and over and over again!"

We have spent several chapters discussing things you need to start doing. Now it's time to switch gears and discuss things that you need to STOP doing (as soon as possible) if you want to be more productive, more purposeful and, yes, happier.

Stop hitting the snooze button!

Now this may seem counter-intuitive, since I just spent an entire chapter telling you that you need to get plenty of sleep so your brain can function at its highest level. You do need to get plenty of sleep. But once it's time to wake up, get up.

Look, we all know the practical implications. We set the alarm clock the night before. We picked that alarm time because we had a lot to do and 6:30am (for example) would give us plenty of time to get everything done. It would get our day off on the right foot.

But then, when that alarm goes off, it's just so damn hard!

The bed has never seemed so warm and comfortable, so we hit that snooze button for just a few more minutes of glorious sleep. And let's face it, once you do it once, it's easier to hit that button a second time…and a third.

Then we wake up with the realization that there is no way we can get everything done AND make it to work on time. So, we rush around, do everything half-assed, and the productive morning we planned is shot.

Sound familiar? Yeah...me too. This sort of hectic beginning to your day is exactly the wrong way to live intentionally.

But there's more to it than that.

Have you ever noticed that when you do hit the snooze button, you never seem to feel more rested? According to Mel Robbins in the *5 Second Rule* (yes, I love that book), it's because of the way our bodies deal with sleep.

You see, we sleep in 90-minute cycles. A sleep cycle lasts about 90 minutes, and during that time we move through five stages of sleep. The first four stages make up our non-rapid eye movement (NREM) sleep, and the fifth stage is when rapid eye movement (REM) sleep occurs. As the evening comes to a close, and our body starts to get ready to wake, we enter a 2-hour cycle to prepare for the day.

This is where we are when our alarm goes off. We are ready to wake up. We may not feel like it (right away) but this is the ideal time to launch.

What happens when we hit the snooze button? Though we think we are just laying back down to get "nine more minutes," our bodies don't get the memo. As you fall back to sleep, your body enters into another 90-minute sleep cycle again!

That is why it is so hard to wake back up when the snooze button goes off again! You think you are giving your body a bit more rest, but you are actually programming yourself to be more tired throughout the morning...and it jacks with your cycle for the rest of the day!

It's simple. It's just not easy. You know what to do. For tomorrow, let's start with the basics. Put your alarm clock across the room, so you have to put your feet on the floor to turn it off. When your alarm starts to sound, get out of bed to make it stop!

Now that you are up...start your day.

Look, I get it. Like everything else in life, it sounds easy as you are reading it. In practice, it's much harder. But now you have the practical science, hitting the snooze button is holding you back.

Stop. Hitting. The. Snooze. Button.

CHAPTER 18

STOP MULTI-TASKING

"Research shows that, in addition to slowing you down, multitasking lowers your IQ."
Dr. Travis Bradberry

I have been blessed to have had the opportunity to speak to many people over the past several years about productivity. I love doing it. I really enjoy talking with people about things they should start and stop if they want to be more productive.

And when it comes to this portion of the talk, I always ask the group, "How many of you are great at multi-tasking? Raise your hand."

At this point they should really see Admiral Ackbar's face from *Return of the Jedi*. As a few poor souls proudly raise their hands he would be yelling at them, "It's a trap!"

No one is good at multi-tasking. No...you are not. It's not my opinion. It's the way the brain works.

You see, when it's operating well, the human brain is an amazing tool. It moves so fast (most of the time) that it feels like we can switch from task to task while chewing gum and humming a Taylor Swift song, and never miss a beat. It might FEEL that way, but it's not what is happening. What is really happening is that with each change of task, our brain has to stop what it is focusing on, change tasks and start up again. Again, often this seems to happen quickly. But it is a total killer for productivity.

It can even be a killer in real life. Texting and driving are actually illegal! Why? Because, seriously, it KILLS people!

Now sometimes I get some push back on this. Let me address a few.

But I CAN do two things at the same time!

Let me clarify a bit there. You can do two mindless activities at the same time. You can walk and chew gum (well, most of you can). But what you cannot do is FOCUS on two things at the same time. You can't think deeply about one thing and work on another effectively. It's the reason when you feel lost in traffic and you don't know where to go, you often instinctively turn down the radio. "That's enough Taylor! I need to focus." Don't worry about it. Haters gonna hate.

I really AM good at multi-tasking!

I hate to break it to you, but if you think you are good at multi-tasking, you are probably actually worse! Studies show that those who are confident in their multi-tasking abilities often do worse on productivity tests. Their overconfidence gets the best of them!

But I am a woman. We are better at multi-tasking!

Great news ladies! You are right. Women are slightly better at multi-tasking than men. Maybe it's evolution. Maybe it's genetics. But most studies show women have a slight edge. But make no mistake ladies... you are still not good at multi-tasking. The science is just the same. It just means you suck slightly less at it. It's still absolutely the worst way to get more accomplished.

What is interesting to me is that this is probably the most studied of my "stop" activities. There is study after study after study proving this to be true. Multi-tasking absolutely, without a doubt, decreases our effectiveness. But it's also the one that is hardest for many people to let go. Everyone seems to think that they are the exception to the rule, or that all the science is wrong.

They are not wrong. Multi-tasking kills productivity.

If you want to feel more purposeful, less harried, and get more done, you need to STOP multi-tasking today.

"Okay," you might be thinking. "I get it and I want to get better. But how do I stop multi-tasking?" Here are a few tactics.

Turn Off Alerts: Our phones are amazing tools for productivity when we use them as a tool. But so often, we create a world where they drive the bus...not us. Most of the time, you do not need to know every time you get an email. You should not care every time you get a Facebook notification. There are a few that really matter. But honestly, most of them do not. Turn off your notifications and check in when you want to. You will be wonderfully surprised how freeing this is.

Schedule/Calendar Block: There are activities in your day that require more deep thinking. It's as simple as making sure those make the calendar. Schedule time to write or make prospect calls. Those things that are most important for your success should be on your calendar. Put them there and keep that date with yourself.

Batch Activities: Some activities in your day are very similar, and once you get in the mindset you can really keep rolling. But if you get distracted, it's hard to get back in the groove. For me, I love to write or make sales calls or be creative. But if I get a call to discuss a finance issue, it is REALLY hard for me to get back on track. So, I try to schedule so I can get a lot of things done in a batch. This helps to keep me from bouncing back and forth from one thing to another.

In other words, it keeps me from multi-tasking.

CHAPTER 19

STOP COMPARING (TO OTHERS)

"Comparison is the thief of joy."
Theodore Roosevelt

My wife and I were on a walk. On warm summer evenings, when schedules allow, we enjoy catching up this way. It's an opportunity to get our blood flowing and find out what each of us is working on. She is a great sounding board for me, and I love hearing her opinions on what I am working.

On this particular walk, we started talking about friends that were on vacations. It was that "season," when it seemed that everyone we knew was filling up our Facebook feed with their beautiful beach pictures. One friend, in particular we commented, seemed like he was perpetually on vacation! What cruise ship was he on now? Before long, our well-intentioned comments turned to jealousy.

Why can't we go on vacation all of time? Why do they have so much time? Why don't we have more money?

Comparing your life to others has been around forever. The term "Keeping up with the Joneses" is not new. And though, for the most part, I really like Social Media, it takes this to a new level. We have the ability, at every given second in our lives to see how great everyone else seems to have it.

All our friends seem to have perfect kids, and perfect marriages, and Instagram filtered lives. We, on the other hand, seem to be leading a life that is always on the brink of collapse. We are tired. We don't seem to have enough money to go around. We love our kids, but they are loud! Why does my life not look like their life? What am I doing wrong?

But there is one very important thing to remember.

You are comparing your "behind the scenes" to everyone else's "highlight reel."

Most of us tend to put a very edited version of ourselves on Social Media. That is fine. And frankly it makes sense. But you are looking at everyone else's edit. You are looking at their greatest hits.

But when you look at your own life, you see the messiness. You think of the most recent fight you had with your spouse. You know what your finances really look like. You (and I) know that life is not even close to perfect. Of course, it's not...it never is. And neither is anyone else's!

Comparing your life to others is a joy stealer. It's unproductive and it leads to jealousy. Want a quick hack to help to make it more productive? Start to admire!

Jealousy versus Admiration

When you see someone else having some level of success in life, especially if that success comes in the form of something you want, it's natural to be a bit jealous. They have what you want. You're working hard to chase a dream, and it seems like it's coming easy to them. They are ahead of you on the path. It's natural to ask, "why not me?"

It's also incredibly unproductive.

When faced with a situation like this, re-direct your focus from jealousy to admiration. Jealousy is a negative emotion that shuts down your creative brain. Admiration still shows you the gap between what you want, and what you have. But that change gives your brain the space to not only admire them but learn from them. What are they doing that you are not? Who do they know? What training have they done? What can you learn from them?

When you admire someone, you can learn from them.

Comparing with You

Do you see the hypocrisy? I am telling you to "not compare" yourself with others, while I am also telling you that comparison is natural. It's not a new phenomenon. As humans, we are wired to look around and see differences. Thousands of years ago, we used this ability to keep us alive. Now it just drives us crazy.

But there is one way you can use comparison to your advantage.

If you are a person who is working to grow and evolve in your life (and you are reading a book like this, so you likely are!), then by definition, there will be a gap between where you are now and where you want to be. That's the point of creating the goal!

You want to be more fit, so you set a goal to lose 10 pounds.

You want to make more money, so you set a goal to sell more.

You want to write a book, so you set a goal for writing.

You get the idea. You have a thing you want to accomplish, and you are not there now. There is a gap. Anyone who is aspirational understands. There is a challenge here too, though. As Jeff Haden writes in the *Motivation Myth*, we have to be careful between the "distance between here and there."

Let me explain.

If you are training for a marathon and you are struggling (early in training) with a 2-mile run, you can easily get discouraged. You might say to yourself "I can't even run 2 miles! How will I ever run 26.2?" The distance between here and there just seems too far!

What Jeff urges us to do is to simply focus on the task at hand. You don't need to run 26.2 miles today. Today you only need to run 2 miles. That is the task today. You need to work hard to accomplish THAT task.

Which leads me to the hack in comparing. Stop comparing yourself to others. But along the journey, it can sometimes help to compare yourself today, to you from 3 weeks ago. Often, in the course of doing battle with a goal, you can't see the incremental improvements. But if you take a look at how far you have come, it can really give you a boost. Yes, you still have a long way to go…but look at what you have accomplished so far!

The message in all of this is simple. If you want to be more productive, and frankly WAY happier, stop comparing your journey to everyone else's. You are not on their path and they are not on yours.

On the other hand, comparing you to you might be just the motivation you need to get you back to work!

CHAPTER 20

STOP COMPLAINING

"Any fool can criticize, condemn and complain.
And most fools do."
Dale Carnegie

There is a disease that is rampant in our culture right now. It decreases our happiness and our productivity, and it affects nearly all of the population (at times). We don't know how or when it started, but we think it started with a decrease in gratitude. You can see the symptoms everywhere you look. It's rampant.

It's the disease of complaining.

Complaining is a destroyer of productivity ...and a thief of joy. And here's the thing, even the most joyful person struggles with this sometimes. We might even think it can be helpful! I hear all the time, "I just need to vent!" The idea, of course being, if I just get this off my chest, I will feel better.

But here's a secret. It doesn't help. Let's dig into the reasons you should (try to) cut complaining out of your life immediately.

Complaining begets Complaining

I think one of the challenges with complaining is we think that it's harmless. We think that we can just get something off our chest and move on. But we don't actually just move on. You see, complaining is just like anything else we do over and over in our brain. It creates a neural pathway. The more we do it, the more that pathway becomes stronger. So, the more we complain, the more it becomes easier for our brain to create that as a habit. And just like any other habit, once we create that behavior, it is really hard to stop! So, when you think you are harmlessly venting, you are actually creating habit to make you a lifelong complainer.

It Actually Does NOT Help

So often, we complain or vent because we feel like if we "get it off our chests" we will feel better and help us move on. Studies are actually starting to show that is not the case. It seems that those who were allowed to complain or scream or punch a punching bag (all things designed to release frustration) actually made study participants MORE aggressive later. So, the very thing you think is making you feel better, is likely making you angrier.

You Are Part of the 90%

Studies tell us that approximately 89% of the world around us is negative. We are surrounded by it. It's the reason we have to be so intentional about being positive. So, when you complain, you just contribute to the muck.

It Doesn't Fix the Problem

The problem I have with most complaining is that it is completely devoid of solution. Most people want to bitch and moan about the problems that they see in their company, family or community. But they really don't want to do anything to make them better. They have no (real) suggestions, and if they do, they don't want to actually work on them. That, my friends, is the definition of a waste of time.

Takes Us Away From the Present

In the book *Solve For Happy*, Mo Gawdat talks about the importance of being in the present moment if you want to experience more joy. Gawdat points out that nearly all negative emotions in our lives are rooted in either the past or the future. We are angry about something that happened yesterday or worried about something that could happen tomorrow (go ahead, think about it). What this does is take us away from our present moment. The most positive and productive people do one thing really well. They live in the "now."

Look, in the interest of transparency, this is really hard for me too. In many ways, complaining comes very natural to us all. You should not beat yourself up if you catch yourself doing this from time to time. But the important thing here is the phrase "from time to time." It is really easy to take it from occasionally to always.

We all know that person who is mad if they cannot find something to be pissed off about!

It's time to shine a light on complaining. It steals your happiness. If you want a simple trick to break the cycle, consider taking a gratitude challenge. When you find yourself "needing to vent", take a breath and consider something that makes your grateful. It can replace that negative emotion with one that can give you joy.

Regardless of how you do it, it's time to take action.

Stop. Complaining.

Please...

CHAPTER 21

STOP MAKING EXCUSES

If it is important to you, you will find a way.
If not, you will find an excuse.

In every organization and in every circle of life, there is that one person. It's the person who has the talent, the skill, the smarts, and the looks to create success in their life...but they don't. The ability is there. They seem to know what they want (and often they talk a lot about it). But for some reason, they just can't seem to get over the hump.

Or you might know this person. They are the person in your life who always has a lot of ideas. With each idea, they are excited and passionate and (seemingly) knowledgeable. For the first few ideas, you might even encourage them. "Sure," you say, "that sounds like an interesting idea! Go make it happen!" But then they don't. And soon they have a new, shiny idea that they are telling you about.

Why don't these people ever execute? Why aren't they able to create some level of success? Why can't they stick with something long enough to see it through?

Most of the time the reason is simple: excuses.

That may sound harsh, but excuses are the downfall of many an idea. And let's face it, it's not just with the mythical person that I just described above. It's with me. It's with you. Most of the time, excuses are the things that are holding us back in any area of our life. (It's the reason I created this entire section of the book). We need to get rid of excuses in our life if we want to grow.

Oh, and they are EASY to see in other people! When our friends point to why they are not able to achieve their goals, we see excuses as the insidious beasts that they are!

But when it comes to our own excuses, we have a different name for them.

We call them *REASONS*.

I don't have time to work out. Nearly all of us could create 30 minutes in our day.

I don't have the money/resources to start that new business. But yet thousands of startup ventures have been created on a shoestring budget.

You get the idea. In any area of our life where we are not reaching our full potential (and I certainly have mine), we are being held back by excuses.

That's why I really like what entrepreneur, author and real estate investor, Grant Cardone, has to say about this. He says that he takes responsibility for EVERYTHING in his life. No matter what happens in his business or in his life, it's his fault.

Late for work? That's his fault. He could have left earlier.

Didn't get the sale? Totally on him. He could have pitched better, done more research, etc.

Got rear-ended in traffic? Yep...he takes the credit.

This is not just martyr mentality. He is not doing this just to stroke his ego. The idea is simple. If you are looking to blame someone else in every situation, that is what your brain will do. It will come up with someone (other than you) that holds responsibility for your situation. If you eliminate excuses, you will start to see how you can affect areas in your life in a positive way.

I love this idea. Not only do you start to learn something from every situation (and trust me, that is the point), you also completely get rid of the idea of being a victim. When everything is up to you, you have the ability to learn something from every situation. This is not being a martyr. On the contrary, I find it very empowering.

It is the opposite of helpless. It is a mentality that says, "I always can make a difference. I can always make it better."

So, let's take a second and think about an area in your life where you are coming up short. What are the excuses you are giving yourself? (I know. I know. They are reasons!) What could you accomplish if you could remove the blame game? What do you do if you got rid of the obstacles in your way?

How would you feel?

It's simple. It's not easy. It's time to STOP making excuses.

CHAPTER 22

STOP PART-TIMING

"A person being too busy is a myth. People make time for things that are really important to them."
Mandy Hale

The word busy is the most over-used word in our culture today. People walk around talking about how "busy" they are as if it is a badge of honor to be worn on their chest. It's become so ubiquitous that it's a response to any question!

How are you? Busy.

How is the family? Busy.

My friends, busy is NOT the point. The goal is not to fill up your calendar with the most amount of activities. I hope this book has helped you understand that the goal is not to be busy. The goal is to be productive! The goal is to push out good. The goal is to provide value and live a life that you are passionate about.

You can't do that if you are just "too busy."

I'll let you in on a little secret. You are not too busy. You are Part-Timing. Your calendar is (probably) full of things that you are not that excited about. And since you have a calendar that is full of things you are "meh" about, you don't have room for the things that truly matter.

Derek Sivers talks about this in his book, *Anything You Want*. Derek created the website CD Baby back before everything was available on the internet. He created a wildly successful company before selling to Yahoo. And what he found was, the more successful he got, the more requests he received. You see, once people see you as successful, the more they want you to help with their project.

That's a great thing! You get the opportunity to see and work on some really cool projects. The problem is most of us are really bad at one thing…saying no. While it's great to be invited to all these projects, not all of them are things you are passionate about. So, if you're not careful, you're going to fill your calendar with things you are "meh" about. You are not against them. You are fine with them. You are just not that excited about them. So, you end up with a calendar full of crap you don't care about.

That's why Derek created this rule about projects he was invited to work on.

"If it's not a 'Hell yes', it's a no."

This has been one of the most powerful (and hard to follow) rules in my life. Here's the thing, if the answer is "hell yes" that means it's a project you are fired up about! You will happily move other stuff off your calendar in order to focus on it. It's not a problem to "make the time." You want to! The thing is though, there are not many things that make you feel like that! Most things that you are approached about are not "hell yes." The answer to these projects usually falls under the category of "sure" or "ok" or "I guess." And if you feel yourself with these answers in your head (or in your gut) then you need to say, "No."

I just want to acknowledge that this is really hard. Like you, I don't want to hurt anyone's feelings. To them, the project they want you to work on is a "hell yes." They are probably really passionate about it! But here's the thing, if you are not, you will likely do a crappy job helping them anyway. You won't want to attend that meeting. You won't want to make those calls.

You will Part-Time it. And Part-Timing it is how most people go through life. Their calendar is absolutely chock full of things they don't really care about. And it shows.

So, my final STOP for you is simple. It's time to STOP Part-Timing your life. You need to figure out the projects in your life that you are completely fired up about. You also need to take the time and look at the things that are "energy suckers" on your calendar. You know the ones. They're the meetings you hate going too. They are the people whose calls you don't want to answer.

Now take your energy suckers off your calendar. Gracefully bow out. Wish them luck. Be kind. But give yourself the gift of being passionate about what you want your life to be. Work on those things (as much as you can).

Stop. Part-Timing.

CHAPTER 23

GET MORE STUFF DONE... TACTICS

It's time to roll up your sleeves...and get after it!

If you have made it this far, congratulations! You are well on your way to creating success in our *Give First Economy*. It takes work. It takes time. But as we have talked about here in Part 2 of the book, you need to be able to get things done. It won't just come to you.

When I attend a conference, listen to a podcast or read a book, I like to have some things that I can implement immediately. That's why I wanted to finish up Part 2 of the book with some tactical things you can do to get more done...and lean into the project you are passionate about.

Let's dig into some tactics of **Getting More Done**.

Lift the Heavy Stuff First

The first time I was big enough to help my dad move something, he taught me a valuable lesson. We looked at a room full of furniture that my Mom wanted moved around and he went straight to the heaviest thing in the room. I was not excited. But he explained, "Always lift the heavy stuff first. When you get that out of the way, everything else will seem easier."

Not only is that GREAT advice when moving your friends, it's true when planning your day too. The thing that you need to do the most is often the thing that gets put off. Do that first... the rest of your day will seem easier.

Create a Support Team

The best people don't go it alone. It's up to us for sure. But it's important to have a great support team. That might not mean a staff. It might just be a group of people that help push you.

But it's important to be intentional about this group. We have all heard that we are the average of the 5 people we hang around with most. Make sure you have people that lift you up…those are important. But don't forget to have people that are willing to call you out (with good intentions) when you are not giving your best. Get the right people on your support team!

Fill Your Calendars with the Most Important

At one point a few years ago, I had too much on my plate. I was distracted and was not giving anything my best. (I was Part-Timing). So, I met with my team at Hasseman Marketing and said, "What do I do that brings the most value to the company?" We spent some time discussing this and they came up with 3 things. I brought the most value when I was doing sales (meeting with customers and prospects), creating content and training the rest of our sales team. That's it… those 3 things. I looked at my assistant and said, "Let's make sure my calendar is full of those 3 things." Not only did I become immediately more effective, but it also re-energized me. I was working on the things that mattered!

Touch It Once

This is an oldie but a goodie. Most of us get an email that we intend to get back to when we "have more time to think about it." We know what happens. That email sits on our desk for a week while we think the perfect answer will come. Most of the time, our immediate response is the one we end up with anyway. Just respond now.

Batch Activities

When we bounce from activity to activity, we are forcing our brain to switch back and forth…and it's inefficient. When you can, put similar activities together. Writing a blog? Block out some time and write several. One of the most prolific podcasters in the world is John Lee Dumas. He posted a podcast EVERY DAY for nearly 2000 days in a row! How did he do it? He batched those podcasts every half hour for a full day! He was often able to knock out a full week of content in one day because he batched them together!

Put It On The Calendar (Then Figure It Out)

I was talking with my assistant Em, (who is the real superstar behind my productivity) and told her to reach out to a client that I had not seen in a while. I wanted to schedule a meeting. She asked me "What do you want to meet about?" and I told her, "I don't know yet."

What I did know is I need to spend time in front of certain clients. If I put that activity on the calendar, I would spend the mental time to make sure it was valuable. If I did not schedule that activity, it would never happen.

Don't wait for inspiration to strike. Don't wait for the perfect time. Schedule it...then figure out what you need to do!

These are a few "down and dirty" tactics that help to get me on track when I feel like I am not hitting on all cylinders. I hope they help you!

Now it's up to you. You know what to do. You know how to do it. Now you just need to take action!

Let's get out there and **Give** our way to success!

CHAPTER 24

BOOKS TO READ TO DIG DEEPER

Over the last several years, I have read lots of books about how to market better, sell more, create more dynamic content and how to be an overall better person. Some of these books have been tough to get through, some have been amazing, but I was able to take something from nearly all of them.

But in order to help you get to "the best of the best" quickly, here is a list of books that I have loved and that have impacted me over the past few years. These books come from various areas of interest. Some of them are personal development focused, while others are for entrepreneurs. Please feel free to check out the list and dig into the topics that interest you!

Mindset by Carol Dwek: If you have not read this book, start here. In this book Dr. Carol Dwek explains that there are really only two mindsets; fixed and growth. And your Mindset, can unknowingly determine the overall trajectory of your life. This is powerful and is a must read for anyone that wants to get better...at anything.

7 Habits for Highly Effective People: I recommend this book a lot. That's because I find myself quoting it all the time, and it's been years since I read it. There are so many foundational principles in it that can help anyone. If you want to improve, then be pro-active, stay in your circle of influence, and sharpen the saw by reading this book!

The 5 Second Rule: This is a great book to get you un-stuck. It's a simple principle...but simple does not always mean easy. And if you are going to get this one, I recommend the audiobook because the author Mel Robbins is awesome on it.

The Happiness Equation: I found this one easy to read and a pleasure to learn. Your mind functions better when you feed it "happy." Author Neil Pasricha explains the "hows" and the "whys" in this great book.

Fan of Happy: Okay, you have to give me this one. It's a book about personal development that I (quite literally) wrote for my daughters. **You can check it out on Amazon.**

E-Myth by Michael Gerber: This, my friends, is THE entrepreneur book. It starts here for me. I have read this book 10 times, and every time I read it, I am in a different place in my entrepreneurial journey. It's an easy read and it's powerful.

Profit First by Mike Michaelowicz: For me, this book was a game changer. I listened to this book the first time, and I was honestly wondering if Mike was following me around! We changed the way we did accounting in my business because of this book…and we are glad we did!

Finish by Jon Acuff: If you are like most entrepreneurs I know, you don't have a problem starting new things. But do you finish? Jon Acuff gives tips and tactics for moving things to the "done pile."

Content Inc by Joe Pulizzi: Yes…this is a marketing book. But I think this book has great meaning to entrepreneurs trying to tell their story in the world today. How can you become a "media company?" Start by reading this.

SCRUM by Jeff Sutherland: This book helps to answer the question, "how can my team and I get more done?" The SCRUM methodology is incredibly interesting and allows you to think about project management in a totally different way.

The Automatic Customer by John Warrillow: This one got me thinking about how you can make ANY business a subscription model. I love books that make me think! This one had me running new ideas in my mind for weeks.

4 Disciplines of Execution by Chris McChesney and Sean Covey: If you have ever gone to an event and come back inspired, then watched your ideas get lost "in the whirlwind" of business, this is the book for you. It greats down the 4 steps to implement "wildly important goals."

The Go Giver by Bob Burg and John David Mann: We always here that you need to be a "go getter" to be successful. I love this take on giving first.

The Subtle Art of Not Giving a F*$k by Mark Manson: I loved Mark's take on life. And once you get through the f-bombs, it's pretty zen. My favorite concept had to do with the idea of "what are you willing to suffer through?" No one wants to run 18 miles. But people are often "willing to suffer through it" to run a marathon. I love that.

The Motivation Myth by Jeff Haden: Jeff is a great writer and I love his take on motivation. The best and most successful people don't wait to be struck with motivation. They create their own motivation by doing the little things necessary to move forward every day.

There are quite a few books here but this hardly an exhaustive list. Please feel free to email me with your favorite books at *kirby@hassemanmarketing.com*. Each of us gets better from learning from others. I hope this helps you take the next step in your journey... whatever that journey may be!

CONCLUSION

We have covered a lot of ground a lot of tactics in this book. There have hopefully been a few moments that have made you think. But, in reality, there are probably been quite a few moments that have caused you to think "yeah…I knew that."

I understand. Some of these concepts are simple. But implementing them in our day to day lives is not always easy.

I wish I could give you a list of 5 steps to implement all of these changes. But it doesn't really work like that. What I find is that when I am doing one of these strategies well, I might be falling short on another.

So where do you begin?

My guess is, during the reading of this book you had a couple of "aha" moments. You might have realized, in that moment, that this aha moment was a place you needed to improve.

My suggestion is that you pick one area from each part of the book…and start improving there. If you try to do all of this at one time, you will fail. Pick an area (like giving out Joy) and work hard to do that for one month. Then rinse and repeat. Do the same for an area of "getting more done."

As you get stronger in each of these areas, you will start to see noticeable and measurable results in your life. When that happens, please let me know. Nothing would make me happier than to find out that this helped you take your life, your productivity, your business and your happiness to the next level.

But no matter what you choose to do...act. Though we grow from reading books, nothing really changes without taking the action they suggest. Be one of the people that cause change. Be one of the influential few that choose themselves. Don't wait for someone to give you permission.

It's up to you. Go get it.

GOOD LUCK!